THE
CHAMPION
SPORTS
PARENT

THE
CHAMPION
SPORTS
PARENT

Practical Wisdom for Raising Confident,
Competitive, Mentally Tough Athletes

JERRY LYNCH AND JOHN O'SULLIVAN

THE CHAMPION SPORTS PARENT

Practical Wisdom for Raising Confident, Competitive, Mentally Tough Athletes

ISBN: 978-1-7343426-5-9 paperback
ISBN: 978-1-7343426-6-6 ebook

Library of Congress Control Number: 2024917669

Changing the Game Project
60643 Thunderbird
Bend, Oregon, 97702

www.ChangingTheGameProject.com

Cover Design by: Jonathan Sainsbury
Interior Design by: Laura Jones-Rivera, lauraflojo.com

To my extraordinary mother, Kathleen O'Sullivan (1936–2024), who passed away during the writing of this book. She was always my #1 fan, loved me unconditionally no matter what the score, and always told me, "I love watching you play." She was beautiful. I miss you every day, Mom.

—John

To all parents who truly desire to powerfully and positively influence the sports experience of children. And to all sports children, who give their parents the honor, privilege, and opportunity to truly learn and discover how to be the best version of themselves as parents.

—Jerry

Your kids' success or lack of success in sports does not indicate what kind of parent you are. But having an athlete that is coachable, respectful, a great teammate, mentally tough, resilient, and who tries their best is a direct reflection of your parenting.

—Unknown

CONTENTS

Part III: Coaches Are Your Allies, Not Your Adversaries

Part IV: Game Day Champion Parent Behaviors

INTRODUCTION:

THE DANCE OF SPORTS PARENTING

If you want to help your children to succeed in sports or anything else for that matter, offer support, love, and perhaps more than anything, the space to experience and learn on their own. Maybe by sitting back, enjoying the game, observing your kids in action, you can help them learn the game faster and enjoy it more. Just a thought.
　　　　　　　　—Steve Kerr, head coach, Golden State Warriors

A few years back, John was enjoying a game of golf in his hometown of Bend, Oregon, and was paired with a father and son for his round. The boy was about 14, and he could hit a ball really well. Long, nice draw, great iron play, and pretty good around the green. The kid was a solid 14-year-old golfer.

Hole after hole they played, and the boy was scoring much better than his dad and John, despite the coaching his father was constantly giving him.

"Keep your head down," after an errant drive.

"You were supposed to be right of the flag there—come on, son," as the boy hit his approach shot to the wrong part of the green.

"Stay focused!" after the boy misread a putt.

"He's pretty good," said John after the boy smashed another drive down the middle of the fairway.

"We're thinking of packing up and moving cross-country to Florida where he can play more golf," the dad said proudly. "It's going to be hard to sell our house, and hopefully I can get a new job; otherwise his mom and I will take turns with him down there while the other one stays here with his siblings. But those are the sacrifices you make when your kid has PGA Tour potential."

"PGA Tour potential?" said John, his eyes a little wider at this point. "You're picking up and moving your whole life and family for your son's golf at age 14?"

"Yeah, I know it sounds nuts," said the father a little sheepishly. "But everyone says if we don't do this now and get him more golf and better coaching, he's going to miss his window."

There were a million and one thoughts racing through John's mind at that point—namely that there were a lot of great golf courses and golf teachers in Bend, that children only get one childhood, and that parents spend 90 percent of their lifetime of hours with their children prior to their 18th birthday, so why give that up? As an author and professional speaker who travels the globe speaking about youth sports, coaching and parenting young athletes, John also knows quite a few top golf coaches, and they will all tell you that players with pretty swings and solid ball striking are a dime a dozen—it takes a lot more than that to make it on tour. John also knew that parents living vicariously through their son's sports often spoil the child's love of sport. There were a lot of things John wanted to say, but the only words that came out were "I wish him luck. He seems like a nice kid."

This is youth sports 2024. It's far too often an over-commercialized, adult-centric enterprise with children and parents trying to keep up with the Joneses, afraid to miss out, many times sacrificing the child's physical health and mental well-being in pursuit of some far-fetched future goal at the behest of coaches and sports organizations charging thousands of dollars for selling the dream. Author

Michael Lewis compared the business of youth sports to the market for addictive drugs: unregulated, fueled by money, and populated by desperate actors.[1] It is often a race to nowhere with both children and parents, in the end, broken-down, beaten, and wondering, *Why did we do that?*

Youth sports is big business. In 2019, the youth sports industry was valued at $19.2 billion, an increase of more than 90 percent from 2010 and over $4 billion more valuable than the NFL. Local sports have disappeared and been replaced by travel leagues and extensive sports tourism. A 2019 Harris Poll of 1,001 adults with children in private sports clubs found that 27 percent paid more than $500 per month on their children's sports. Eight percent paid over $12,000 per year. And sadly, 36 percent of these families took less family vacations, and nearly 20 percent added a second job to help pay the expenses. The sports industrial complex is bleeding families dry, and excluding many other kids who cannot afford to even play.[2]

Perhaps author Linda Flanagan says it best in her wonderful book *Take Back The Game.* "Thanks to the extravagant investment in kids sports, parents' Olympian commitment to their children's recreation, and the exalted role of athletics in higher education," she writes, "much of what we love about youth sports - and why we want our children to play –, has been eroded."[3] We must do better.

We could go on and on about today's youth sports environment, but that is not the purpose of this book. The purpose of this book is to help you, the reader, be the best possible sports parent you can be. Why did we need to write a book?

Because it's hard to be the parent of a young athlete in the 21st century. Harder than it has ever been, and certainly harder than it was

---

1 Linda Flanagan, *Take Back the Game: How Money and Mania Are Ruining Kids' Sports—and Why It Matters* (New York: Penguin Portfolio, 2022), xviii.

2 Flanagan, *Take Back the* Game, 10–17.

3 Flanagan, xix.

when we were growing up. You will never get it all right, and you will often screw it up. We know this firsthand.

Jerry's youngest son, Brennan, was a top distance runner in the state of California. He came within three seconds of being the state cross country champion and received a scholarship to one of the top running schools in the country, the University of Colorado. Being an accomplished runner himself, Jerry saw how his son was living the dream he never got to experience as a collegiate athlete. He started to live his life, unintentionally, through Brennan's successes and became quite overzealous in the process, much to his embarrassment—and his son's as well. At the time, Jerry, a practicing sport psychologist with 30 years' experience, was looking for purpose and meaning in his athletic life, and Brennan's journey fulfilled what he had hoped to be in college.

One day, as Jerry yelled and screamed instructions from the side of the race course, Brennan stopped running, turned around, and told his dad to zip it. Jerry was mortified as he realized what had been happening—that he had made his son's journey his own. As Jerry says today, "I'm happy to say I am still a bit embarrassed by this, but I'm thrilled that I woke up and learned my lesson that I needed to find my own purpose and simply support him from a distance."

John, too, has had numerous instances of far-from-perfect sports parenting. One in particular he shared in his 2014 TEDx Talk, "Changing the Game in Youth Sports." When his son TJ was only five years old and playing his first soccer game, John was his coach. He was so proud and excited that his son was going to play the sport he loved so much and had made a life out of coaching. Come game time, though, TJ turned to his dad and said, "I don't want to play." John was mortified, embarrassed, and a tad angry. TJ, on the other hand, was perfectly happy, for he had found a lizard on the side of the field to play with. As they got into the car post-game, John couldn't help himself, in spite of all the advice he gave to others through his work. "So TJ . . ." he began, before his wife poked him from the passenger seat.

"Really," she admonished him, "you are going to give him a lecture on the ride home about not playing today? Didn't you write a book about this already?"

We all can lose it from time to time with only the best intentions of helping our children. This book is not about perfect parenting. It's about, as Steve Kerr says in the opening quote, offering them love and support in a fun, joyful environment and the space to learn on their own. Our job is to nudge and encourage forward movement and then get out of the way.

Being a sports parent is an art—a dance—yet it is difficult. Perhaps that's a massive understatement. It can often be demanding, burdensome, and at times, may seem like a horrendous nightmare. Once your children's lives become involved with sports, your own life takes a huge turn, one that often approaches chaos. Getting kids to and from practice demands proficiency in a new profession, one of being a full-time, on-demand chauffeur. Then there are the out-of-town travel events that decimate your weekends. There is the enormous cost of the more competitive teams. Arranging for individual coaching sessions, treating injuries, fundraising, and working the snack bar with all the unhealthy food becomes anathema to your sanity.

However, you must not forget that this sacred journey can also be the most rewarding period of your life. Writing this book is our attempt to set the stage for making this time in your life an extraordinary experience. Our deepest intention is to provide a useful, easy-to-read, practical manual that will help you to 1) implement a more aware, conscious level of parenting as well as 2) guiding you to raise true champions capable of being the best version of themselves by learning invaluable lessons—not only about sports but about life as well.

So why are we the right people to write this book? From the high performance and consulting side of things, we are proud to have been intimately connected with building and sustaining more than 100 world, national, and conference championship cultures. These include

NCAA programs at Stanford, Ohio State, Harvard, UConn, Georgetown, Iowa, Syracuse, Maryland, Duke, North Carolina, Rutgers, Middlebury, Amherst, Colby, and the US Naval Academy, as well as our professional sports involvement with coaches and athletes in the NBA, NFL, NHL, MLS, NLL, and PGA Tour. Fifty-five of our teams have made it to an NCAA Final Four. Numerous teams in Olympic sports and high school and club levels of athletics have experienced the power of our culture, performance, and leadership approach as well.

But perhaps more importantly, we are parents. We have seen our children enjoy the highest of highs and lowest of lows on their sporting journey. Jerry has four kids in their thirties, while John's oldest is now in college and his youngest is a senior in high school. We have seen the youth sports journey to its conclusion, spending nights in the ER and long days in the car traveling to and from games. We have watched our children get injured, beaten down, humiliated, and more. We have watched them cry after great disappointments and make life-long friends through sports. And while we realize that our children are not your children and our experiences are not your experiences, the principles and ideas in this book are ones we have researched, written about, and used with other people's children. Through trial and error, we've found what worked for our kids and what didn't. As author Paulo Coelho says, "The secret of life is to fall seven times and to get up eight times."[4] We have certainly done that with our own children.

No doubt that if you found this book, there are certain things you already do very well, while other things can be improved. As lifelong learners, we all seek ways to add to our skill set and expand our levels of effectiveness. Like everyone involved in sports parenting, you probably have times when you feel stagnant or stuck. That's when this book can be your companion along the way to optimize your chances of being a champion sports parent. Your mistakes serve as your invisible teachers, giving you the gift of wisdom. These setbacks guide you along the path

---

4 Paulo Coelho, *The Alchemist* (New York: HarperCollins Publishers, 1993).

of being a more effective parent helping your children to experience a better relationship with their passion.

We all love our sports kids, yet we also are aware of how we can lose touch with what may be best for our prized athletes. It's easy to impose our needs upon them rather than listen to what they want in order to better understand their personal struggles. This book will help you to be better listeners and, as a result, be more respectful and sensitive to their needs—which is how we gain their loyalty, cooperation, love, and appreciation. And this is the only way they will reach their full capacity as athletes and human beings.

Additionally, this book presents a plethora of specific behaviors, characteristics, and attributes that contribute to a healthy, beautifully choreographed dance between parent, child, and coach, one that will preserve the dreams and goals of the child while at the same time help them realize validation, self-reliance, confidence, empowerment, respect, caring, love, and self-actualization. Raise your hand if you don't desire to help your child develop these traits and values. The beauty of athletics is the way it accelerates the process of having our children learn these traits. Athletics provides an opportunity for us as sports parents to learn lessons in a one hour event that normally would take a month, a year, or even a lifetime to absorb without sports.

This book will help you to embellish the faith you have in your child while reducing the unintentional and irrational fears they may experience, fears so common in the world of sports performance. Having faith instead of fear helps them to reduce anxiety in times of crisis. Without fear, your child feels free to step away and risk setbacks because with your help they have learned the value of failure to help them forge ahead.

Following Your Heart

Undoubtedly, you are reading this book because you are a conscious, caring, and loving parent in search of upping your sports parenting game. You want to improve your toolbox so your child can perform their very best. Knowing this, we ask that you have the courage to follow what your heart is telling you and make the changes you need to not only embellish the sports life of your child but also enhance your relationship with them and improve the overall joy in your life. When you do have this courage, magic happens as your children begin to embrace the notion that they can be something other than ordinary.

Know that this sports parenting journey will take some dedication and mindful work. In the words of the iconic Russian author Fyodor Dostoyevsky, "A new philosophy, a new way of life, is not given for nothing. It's acquired with much patience and great effort." Start slowly with small, gradual, incremental steps, and soon you will experience pleasant rewards of progress and exciting positive change over the entire course of your lives. It is a day-to-day process, up and down, forward and back as you continually improve and blossom as sports parents and as good people.

Sports parenting is a delicate balance. It is the art of selflessly serving your children through firm yet kind, gently worded directives that will give your kids a sense of self-worth. Your children will, as a result, be more productive in their sports experience and loyal to you and your service toward them. We know that kindness and service to others creates a spirit of loyalty. It is necessary, however, that you are firm in addition to being selfless and encouraging toward those you guide. There's no need ever to push, force, coerce, or manipulate your children—or anyone else, for that matter.

How to Use This Book

Much like our last book together, *The Champion Teammate*, the book in your hands has been compiled through wisdom gathered through extensive research and writing, involvement with more than 100 championship teams, consultancies with Hall of Fame coaches, nearly 400 interviews on our *Way of Champions Podcast*, and hundreds of clinics and conferences we conduct on the subject of being an exceptional parent, coach, and teammate. The material here has been gathered from numerous authors, sport scientists, psychologists, and coaches with extensive backgrounds working with parents and children in sports. We share stories of world-famous athletes and teams who epitomize each lesson, as well as wisdom garnered from Native American tradition, Eastern wisdom, Christian mysticism, Latin American cultures, and Western psychology.

The book is broken into four parts, and within each part are a series of lessons and ideas that you can use to be a champion sports parent. The four parts are:

PART I: To Be a Better Parent, Be a Better You
PART II: Teaching Your Child the Inner Game
PART III: Coaches Are Your Allies, Not Your Adversaries
PART IV: Modeling Champion Parent Behaviors

At the end of each section, you will find a quote that will be relevant to that chapter's content. Where relevant and important, we also include an affirmation or two that serve as verbal reinforcers of the message in that section. Every chapter will conclude, finally, with a series of questions and/or activities to promote some thought on your part and discussions with your young athletes. We encourage you to record some of your answers and thoughts so you can return back to this guidebook time and again.

In Part I: To Be a Better Parent, Be a Better You, we look first at ourselves as parents. What is motivating our thoughts and actions? Why do we feel excessive pressure to keep up with the Joneses and allow our actions to be guided by FOMO (Fear of Missing Out)? We then discuss how things such as a servant mindset, gratitude, using the RIVER acronym, and embracing both the good and bad on this journey will help you provide a more consistent foundation for your athletic children.

In Part II, we take a deep dive into the inner game. While we are always seeking out newer fancy equipment, technical trainers, and someone to help our kids get physically stronger and faster, we rarely go inside and improve those four inches between the ears. This is the area that can provide huge advantages to athletes who treat the brain as a muscle and learn how to make it stronger, faster, and clearer. You will learn about visualization and mindfulness, how to turn failure into fuel, and the importance of courage when confidence may be lacking.

In Part III, we delve into the coach-parent relationship. Coaches must be our allies, not our adversaries, and if we work on building trust and understanding, and follow some specific guidelines, we can have a great relationship with our coaches that is beneficial to us and our athletes. You will learn how to both know and embrace your role, effectively communicate, help your coach understand your child, when to let go during difficult situations, and when to intervene in dangerous ones.

Finally, in Part IV, we get into modeling champion behaviors on competition days. There are specific things we should and should not do pre-competition, during competition, and post-competition. Adhering to these items will give your child the best mindset to perform before and during the game and create a safe place for them to unwind after it. Ignore them, and you potentially set your child up for failure during their event and misery on the ride home.

Being a Champion Sports Parent

With an open heart and mind, we ask that you embrace this "new" approach of BEING a champion sports parent. Know that you do not BECOME a champion sports parent. You choose to BE one by implementing the behaviors, strategies, observations, tools, and time-honored suggestions we propose in this book. There are no outcomes or results to measure your progress. Progress is accrued intuitively in this very moment measured by your intentions, your purpose, and your desire to make a positive difference in the lives of your children and the kids of other parents. Progress is measured by the smile on your child's face. Progress is measured by the joy experienced before, during, and after the event. Progress is measured by the everyday elevated feelings you and your child experience because sports has now become the way you create family fun, happiness, and value in life. All this is valid, anecdotal data. It's a way of living that feels extraordinary. This is what it means to BE a champion sports parent.

Your First Question

Now, we encourage you to take your first step. Take a few moments and answer this question:

What is the purpose of sports for my child/children?

_____

_____

_____

_____

Knowing why you put your children in sports is critical. Is it to win championships and trophies? Is it to build memories? Is it to reinforce the values and lessons you teach at home, as well as learn to experience adversity, do hard things, and become an active and healthy adult? Only you can answer this question, so give it some time. Come back to it. Because for many people, the sports industrial complex and environment of youth sports pushes children away from the original purpose of sport.

Once you have recorded your answer, dive into the book. Begin to read and implement what you have learned immediately. With renewed enthusiasm, celebrate your youngsters and their athletic experience in the spirit of playfulness. Let sports awaken you to the awesome positive exchange between you and your young stars, this soulful dance of conscious sports parenting. The poet Rumi mentions that "when you do things from your soul, you feel a river moving in you, a joy." We love sports, but what really fills our hearts is knowing that a positive sports experience can inspire and empower your child more than any other experience in life.

PART I:

TO BE A BETTER PARENT, BE A BETTER YOU

The journey of a thousand miles begins with one step.

— Lao Tzu

In the introduction, John shared a story about coaching his son TJ when he was five years old. On that day, when his son decided he did not want to play, John was still a rational, insightful, educated parent. He was simply scared. He was afraid his son was missing out on a game he loved. He was suffering from FOMO: Fear Of Missing Out!

Through the youth sporting journeys of our kids, we've both had FOMO moments. We saw other kids their age who were better players and wondered, *What have I failed to do?* We saw other kids who played only one sport improving more quickly than ours, and we worried ours would fall too far behind. We saw other kids attending additional skill training sessions and summer camps that ours did not, and we worried that our kids may be missing out.

We know we are not alone in feeling this way. We hear from parents all the time who feel stressed and anxious about their child's sports experience. *Are my kids falling behind? If they don't do extra training now, will they make the travel team? Will they make the high school team? Will they have a chance to play in college?* These are very legitimate concerns for the modern-day sports parent. They might even keep you awake at night.

But here's the thing: They are just kids. They are fine. They need to want to do these things, not be forced to. Your child's path is not supposed to be every other child's path. And the most important person on your child's path is you. A healthy, rational, informed parent can be the key to a child's development, while a stressed-out, anxious, over-bearing parent can spell disaster. It starts with you!

In this section of our book, we provide specific, mindful, inspi-rational, insightful, time-honored strategies and tools for helping you to find purpose and personal meaning while guiding your children along the uncharted path of sports parenting. As parents, we all want the best for our young stars and have pure intentions to make this so, yet mistakes will happen. For example, it is a mistake to find your own purpose and meaning through your child's activity. It is their game, not yours, and this section will help you to discover your true role and purpose while parenting your athletes.

The strategies within this part of the book will help you to obtain a better understanding of what this work is all about and how to make the best of the opportunity given to you. The wisdom within these pages is not meant to preach dogma but rather to teach truth. That truth is based on ways we have tested and proven to have a positive effect on your children. This truth can be found in all of life, from ancient teachings from more than 2,500 years ago to the present day as it relates to all levels of sports parenting and performance. Your child participates in sports not to fulfill *your* needs. You participate in sports to fulfill *theirs*. And in the process, you are being a champion sports parent providing an extraordinary experience for your young athletes on and off the field.

CHAPTER 1:

THE NEXT TRAIN TO STANFORD

Your children were not born to complete your life;
they were born to complete their own.
—William Martin, author of *The Parents Tao Te Ching*

Those of us who grew up in the 20th century likely had a very different childhood than our children have today. Growing up in Brooklyn, New York, many years ago, Jerry never saw his parents involved in any of his sport activities. Parents just didn't get involved with athletics. He and his friends would begin a summer day at the schoolyard and play sports nonstop for 12 hours, coming home only for lunch. Yet that same neighborhood produced five professional athletes and many others who went on to achieve national prominence in a variety of sports with no parental involvement. This story is not atypical.

In this profound opening quote, our friend Bill Martin tells us we shouldn't look to our children to provide meaning for our lives—because if we do, our lives will be meaningless. It's perfectly normal to care and want to help your child, yet it's easy to be overly invested in their success. So many of us get caught in the trap of wanting our precious little athletes to "catch the next train to Stanford" as we live vicariously through their achievements. Sound familiar?

We all must discover personal meaning and purpose in the bigger game of life. If we rely on our children for meaning, it conveys the wrong message, and they come to believe that your love is based on their performance. Most of us have no intention to be this way, but we communicate the message in subtle ways that are easily felt by our children. For example, asking the question following an event, "How did you do?" demonstrates your interest in outcome performance. Rather, asking the question, "How do you feel?" or "What was it like?" is easily translated by them as "My parents care about me."

It's important to remember that kids do not play sports for Mom and Dad. Sports are their thing, not ours. If left alone, they play to have fun, caring very little about winning or achieving. Oftentimes kids will lose a game yet claim that it was great and so much fun.

This problem of overzealous parents, while unintentional, is universal. We have written this chapter not as a critique of sports parenting, but simply as a reminder to stay awake and aware of when we lose focus about our purpose as a sports parent. Our purpose is to support, encourage, and listen to what our kids need and simply say, "I love watching you play." My kids loved it when I asked the most important post-event question a parent could ask: "Who wants something to eat?"

Sports parenting, obviously, is a huge challenge. However, it provides us all with an amazing opportunity for authentic, genuine inner growth. The lessons we learn from navigating the athletic journey of our children impact the quality of our personal lives as well. Our young athletes are like Zen masters in residence, teaching us lessons we need but would rather not know. We become aware of what is important to them and mindful of how we must be not just good parents but good friends, partners, and the best people we can be in all of life.

As you continue to read this book, you will find your true purpose and meaning as well as your true self. Your children will feel more confident and self-reliant. They will follow their hearts, make their own decisions, and become well-adjusted adults. Find your purpose and meaning, and they will find theirs.

Children are our greatest teachers. Notice this and learn accordingly.
—Unknown

Questions on the Quest

1. What is the most important lesson you learned from this chapter?
2. How can this lesson be applied in all your relationships?
3. What can you start doing (that you're not doing) to find meaning as a sports parent?
4. What can you stop doing (that you are doing) to find meaning as a sports parent?

CHAPTER 2:

A GOOD SERVANT

It is wise to avoid unnecessarily entering other people's process.
Be unobtrusive and not overbearing. Rarely intervene if possible.
And in this way you serve them well.

—Chinese wisdom

Think of the experience of going to an extraordinary restaurant with exceptional service. The staff is hyper-aware of your needs. If your water glass is low, a server shows up and asks if you need more. If you are finished with your plate, they show up unobtrusively, ask if you are done, and if so, will remove that plate. On the other hand, have you ever experienced the unconscious intrusion of a server thoughtlessly asking how your dinner is as you try to chew a mouthful of food? An aware server will stay in the wings, attuned to your needs, and look for your signals for assistance before entering your space, while a poor server is like a bull in a china shop.

The restaurant analogy is a perfect metaphor for sports parenting. As a champion sports parent, you want to wait in "the wings" of your child's space, letting them determine the appropriate time for you to enter that space. Like a good server, you "set the table" and let them feed themselves.

You must trust your children as they learn how to navigate their sports world—what they need, how they think, what they need to do to experience personal success on their own. Refuse to micromanage their sports lives. You may fear losing control, but when you step aside and get out of their way, paradoxically you gain control. The best farmers have learned that to control their cows, if they move the fences back and give the cows more space, they will never try to run away because they feel freer not being closed in.

If you look through the lens of your children's eyes, parents should be seen and not heard . . . unless, of course, they want to be driven to the mall. Humor aside, kids love knowing their parents are there, but they would rather not have them step in and fix all their problems. They want to make their own decisions and be independent. They desire to be autonomous, and by letting this happen, they will learn to solve problems and develop confidence in themselves. Trust us when we say that your children will let you know when they need help. They need to know you love them and that when needed, you will be there.

This principle will serve you not only as a sports parent, but it will be there when the stakes get even higher as your children get older and need to feel they are free to make life-changing decisions without their parents telling them what to do. It's not easy because you want to protect them. Ironically, though, by being overprotective, you inhibit and stifle their growth into adulthood. Your fear that they may fail is a setup for that failure. If you love them, you will let go and observe them coming to you when they decide the time is right. But they won't do this unless you train them at an early age, especially through sports. Being a good servant to your children is being a good sports parent.

Jerry's children are all in their thirties, and he still finds himself wanting to enter their space, give advice, or even tell them what to do. Perhaps he doesn't listen enough, or maybe he interrupts, and corrects them if he feels they are wrong. This does not work. Before he can catch himself, one of them may say, "Dad, chill out . . . we can handle this." When he hears this, he must remember that they can handle the situation because in their younger years, he taught them to handle struggle, learn from failure, and develop the confidence to say, "We can handle this."

If wishes would come true, more of us would step aside, do less, and let our kids struggle and learn from failure. When we do that, we notice that everything seems to happen as it is supposed to, not as we think it should. Just maybe, our children will be happier, trust us more, and gain a strong inner sense of freedom, thus making our parenting more enjoyable.

> *The sole purpose of life is to serve humanity.*
> —Leo Tolstoy, Russian novelist

Questions on the Quest

1. What is the most important lesson you learned from this chapter?
2. How can this lesson be applied in all your relationships?
3. What can you start doing (that you're not doing) to find meaning as a sports parent?
4. What can you stop doing (that you are doing) to find meaning as a sports parent?

CHAPTER 3:

LEARN TO LISTEN,
LISTEN TO LEARN

Most people do not listen with the intent to understand.
They listen with the intent to reply.
—Stephen R. Covey

Jerry has worked with many national championship teams along with dozens of individual sport athletes who have been national and professional champions. A national class collegiate golf athlete once shared with Jerry what happened when her parents failed to truly listen to her concerns. Feeling the beginning stages of burnout, she told them she wanted time off from the intense training schedule she had experienced since childhood. The parents heard her cry but didn't understand because they didn't listen. As time passed, she became totally disgruntled with the sports scene and dropped out, much to her parents' chagrin. After a period of time, the parents finally realized, albeit too late, that they made the mistake of not listening to their daughter's call for help.

Unfortunately, this story is much too common. Sports kids are not being listened to. There is a huge difference between listening and hearing. Most parents *hear* their children speaking and at the same time, think about how to respond, come up with a solution, or even fix the problem. To reply like this is to not fully understand. We get too concerned about coming up with answers rather than being curious about what we can learn from what we hear. Listening, on the other hand, is an intentional process: You silently ask yourself as your child talks, "What can I learn here?" It is a deep understanding that allows you to ask questions and validate the child's response.

Being a champion sports parent demands that you 1) do a lot of driving and 2) be a good listener. The first one is easy, but the second is more challenging. Why is listening important? When you listen, you send a strong message of caring and love to your children. Listening also demonstrates respect and trust, and as a result, your child feels important, valued, relevant, and empowered. These feelings help your child to function and perform at higher levels in the sports arena and the arena of life.

In Jerry's recent book, *Everyday Championship Wisdom*, he talks about how Duke men's basketball coach Mike Krzyzewski believes that you show someone you care about them by listening. He has said that "there couldn't be any time better spent than listening" to your athletes, staff, family, and friends. When we listen with an open heart, we function with champion wisdom.[5]

It has been said that those who listen with an open heart understand. Listening is one of the most crucial skills a sports parent can develop. Because so many of us feel that we need to talk in order to teach, listening is often overlooked. What I have observed over the years is that the very best champion sports parents are, indeed, good listeners.

---

5 Jerry Lynch, PhD, *Everyday Championship Wisdom: Mindful Lessons in Mastery for Coaching, Competing, and Cohesive Teams* (Comanche, IA: Coaches Choice, 2022), p68.

Learning to improve your listening skill set takes time. Start with asking questions about your child's experiences, concerns, observations, thoughts, and feelings. Then sit back and pay attention to what they say. Ask yourself, "What can I learn here?" and proceed to gain an understanding of what's being said. Hold back on your reply and let go of your need to "fix it"—whatever "it" is.

In fact, "What can I learn here?" can be your go-to phrase to help you stay focused on your intention, purpose, and what's important at the moment. It can allow you to be more present as you create a safe, cooperative, collaborative environment in which learning and growth can thrive.

If you want to further empower, support, gain, and give respect, help others to find answers, solve problems, and make others feel that they count—use what is called *active listening*. Examples of how to listen actively include the following:

- Door openers—an invitation for your child to say more in a noncommittal way; for example, simply saying, "I see."
- Stepping inside the door—an invitation to go further, with expressions like "Tell me more," "I'd like to hear about it," and "Let's discuss it."
- Keeping the door wide open—infinitely more effective. You decode what the real message is; for example, try to understand what the sender is feeling or means. Put into your own words and feedback what you think you hear: "It sounds like," "What I hear you saying is," or "Correct me if I'm wrong."

For active listening to be effective, give feedback only concerning what you feel is your child's message—nothing more, nothing less. Don't warn, moralize, lecture, judge, blame, or criticize. With experience, you will grow more direct and intuitive. For now, simply use what your child says and put it in your own words. At first it may feel contrived or awkward. That's okay; just do it anyway and tell the child that it helps you to understand better. And by the way, if you wish to develop great friendships in your personal life, use active listening as a foundation of your caring and connection.

When you actively listen to your sports children, you help them to feel important, valued, and respected, helping them to go the distance, be loyal, and mentally tougher.
—Steve Kerr

Questions on the Quest

1. What is the most important lesson you learned from this chapter?
2. How can this lesson be applied in all your relationships?
3. What can you start doing (that you're not doing) to find meaning as a sports parent?
4. What can you stop doing (that you are doing) to find meaning as a sports parent?
5. What is the difference between hearing and listening?

CHAPTER 4:

CREATING PREDICTABLE ENVIRONMENTS

Our children are counting on us to provide two things: consistency
and structure. Children need parents who say what they mean,
mean what they say and do what they say they are going to do.
—Barbara Coloroso, bestselling author

Kids love ritual. For the past eighteen years, Jerry's family has enjoyed the consistent and predictable ritual of being together at the same Mexican restaurant every Friday evening. During COVID-19, they chose take-out fare and ate at home. While the food was decent, it was the union of the six of them that formed the habit that continues to this day. The sense of knowing that this will happen creates a security—a structure—that feels safe and fun for all of them.

By ritual, we mean a series of actions performed in a consistent manner whether it is what you say or what you do. Consistency of action in how you speak or what you do translates into comfort and self-reliance. As writer and educator Terry Tempest Williams said,

"Rituals are the formulas by which harmony is restored." Perhaps the most profound aspect of rituals is their power to transform the ordinary into the extraordinary. They are about awakening to the magic and wonder that lies within the most mundane moments.

So it is with being a champion sports parent. Your young stars crave consistency and rituals, especially when it comes to your behavior. This builds confidence and trust in your relationship with your children. As the opening quote suggests, your kids need you to say what you mean, mean what you say, and do what you say you will do. Anything short of this is unsettling and will certainly be reflected in mercurial sports performances of children. Your inconsistent behaviors create inconsistent behaviors with these young athletes both on and off the field.

Kids want environments that are predictable. As they get older, they are able to tolerate less structure and wider boundaries, and when you notice this, adjustments can be made. Love, order, and safety provided by their parents is only possible when life is predictable. Today's sports world tends to be unpredictable, volatile, uncertain, complex, and ambiguous. For this reason alone, we all are in need of consistent and predictable environments. Imagine how your child feels in this insecure world.

To counterbalance this, try to be more consistent in your approach to parenting. Create fun rituals. Avoid erratic behaviors that contribute to their insecurity, tension, and fear. To inspire and empower your youngsters, take accountability for your actions and be dependable when you promise something they are counting on. How you talk with a coach, how you consistently pick up your child each day after practice, and how you volunteer as a team parent all require a sense of comfort and predictability that kids will be aware of at all times.

However, be aware that at times, it may be wise to change things up and not adhere to being consistent when it interferes with a pure intention. Rigidity can be stifling and can interfere with the joy of your child's experience. Ralph Waldo Emerson once said that "foolish consistency is the hobgoblin of little minds." When being consistent interferes with the joy, intention, and purpose of an activity or action, we must examine it carefully and transcend it. For example, when Jerry was a young boy, his mother consistently served dinner at five o'clock . . . every single day. In the summer, he would be having a blast all day in the schoolyard playing a variety of sports games, getting "lost" in the focus on performance and having fun in the process. There were times when he would be late for dinner, and his mom would be outraged and punish him for that. Her consistent habit about dinner interfered with the natural tendency and intention of all kids in summer—to want to be free, play, and explore on one's own.

The key to all this is knowing when consistency serves its purpose to give security, comfort, love, confidence, and trust. This was not the case when Jerry was punished for being five minutes late for a dinner he didn't even want to eat. May we all be more vigilant and mindful and aware about the benefits and advantages of what we create. In this way, you will inspire and empower your children and strengthen the trust bond so necessary for a healthy relationship with them.

Ritual is the act of sanctifying action, even ordinary
action so that it has meaning.
—Christina Baldwin, author of *The Circle Way*

Questions on the Quest

1. What are a few examples of your family rituals? How do they help kids?
2. What is one thing you learned here that you needed to know?
3. What would be a new consistent behavior that would promote comfort for kids?
4. What do you need to start doing (that you're not doing) to create consistency?
5. What do you need to stop doing (that you are doing) to create more consistency?

CHAPTER 5:

DETACHMENT FROM CONTROL

*Letting go gives us freedom, and freedom is the only condition for happiness.
If in our heart we still cling to anything, we cannot be free.*
—Thich Nhat Hanh, Buddhist teacher

Todd Marinovich grew up in Newport Beach, California, the son of Marv Marinovich, a lineman and captain for the USC Trojans during their 1962 national championship season. After seeing his own NFL career cut short by overtraining mistakes, Marv studied Eastern Bloc training methods, nutrition, and flexibility and began using the techniques on his son Todd before he could even walk. Throughout his childhood, Todd ate no sweets, bringing his own cakes to birthday parties to avoid the sugar and processed flour. It all seemed to be working, as Todd was labeled a "robo quarterback" by *Sports Illustrated* as he became a high school football star and committed to play football at USC. Yet behind the scenes, trouble was already brewing.

In order to escape the serious pressure and anxiety caused by his dad's strict regimen, Todd began using drugs and drinking in high school. Despite a successful first year at USC, he struggled as a sophomore and was arrested for cocaine possession. He was eventually drafted into the NFL, but he soon failed numerous drug tests and flamed out as he continued to struggle with substance abuse. He soon turned to heroin and methamphetamines, not only ending his football career, but going to prison nearly a dozen times. Todd is widely considered one of the biggest flops of all time in sports, and it's an incredibly sad story—a story that starts and ends with an all-controlling father living vicariously through his son. And while it started out with awards and accolades, it finished in a prison cell.

While the Todd Marinovich story is an extreme one, it still speaks to the importance of letting your kids drive the bus and giving them ownership and autonomy of their sports experience. The more you try to exert control of your athletic kids, the less control you will have. When you detach from the need to have control, paradoxically you gain it. To be a champion sports parent, you must refuse to micromanage the progress of your children.

So many parents cling to their children's journey out of fear of losing control. We know; we've been there. Parents fear that their kids will struggle and fail. They offer to protect them and as a result, deprive these youngsters the opportunity to develop resilience, fortitude, and courage from falling down and finding a way back up on their own. Clinging to control creates tension, anxiety, and fear that can be felt by your children, and this will interfere with their performance and the joy of playing sports.

You may notice how some parents are overzealous and overbearing at an event and even at practice. One wonders if the cause of this behavior is their belief that they are not doing their job unless they are micromanaging the child's progress, making suggestions to the coach, and telling the athlete how to perform in an attempt to control every facet of the sports experience. We believe that such attempts for control are clear indications of insecurity on the part of these well-intentioned parents. But it all backfires if this insecurity is passed on to the child.

If you want your child to develop self-reliance, fortitude, courage, and self-control, you must let go of control. By doing so, your child will develop their wings to fly, fail, and begin again, getting stronger with each attempt. In this way, they feel free, which provides them with the confidence to ultimately experience their full potential. Young athletes who grow up protected from failure, setback, mistakes, and struggle are at a great disadvantage, unable to develop the inner virtues that will support their journey when you are not around.

Detaching from this control does not imply that you don't care. Detachment means that you let go of measuring your self-worth as a sports parent by the outcomes of your child's journey. You get out of the way of your ego, and as a result, the perspective you gain about the value of the sports experience is healthier and more in line with what matters most: the overall emotional, mental, and spiritual growth of your child.

The Chinese symbol for control emphasizes the way of letting go, a way to give these great spirits loving kindness, guidance, and the space to grow, explore, and discover personal greatness.

You can only lose what you cling to.
—Buddhist thought

Questions on the Quest

1. What specific fears might you have about giving your child too much freedom?
2. How realistic are those fears and what parts are irrational?
3. What can you start doing (that you're not doing) to give up some control behaviors?
4. What can you stop doing (that you are doing) to give up some control behaviors?
5. In what ways do you apply or use unnecessary control? How can that change?

CHAPTER 6:

MOTIVATION IS AN INSIDE JOB

Don't force anything to make it happen.
Allow things to unfold naturally as they are supposed to,
not as we think they should. If it is meant to be it will be.

—Chinese wisdom of *wu wei*

One of Jerry's kids, Sean, was an outstanding national class basketball athlete from a very young age. One day during his sophomore year in high school, he announced that he did not want to pursue basketball any further, much to Jerry's chagrin. Fortunately, Jerry had the sense to listen to Sean's wishes (a rare occasion for Dad). Two weeks later, Sean was ready and motivated to return to the team for reasons his family did not know.

Sean went on to win the state championship, and today he is a head basketball coach at a junior college in California because he had a safe environment to decide what he wanted for himself. Creating this kind of safe environment is one of the more powerful ways to accelerate the readiness factor.

The champion sports parent demonstrates flexibility and yields to the desires of their children if they don't seem ready to move forward, which can be the case for young athletes who appear not to be measuring up to their potential or seem unmotivated and unwilling to do the work required by the coach.

All kids are different, and we need to recognize this fact when guiding them effectively. Observe the differences in children especially when it entails a readiness quotient. Many of us struggle with our children's motivation to advance, but that motivation must come from within . . . motivation is an inside job and when they're ready, they will move forward because they want to, not because you want it for them. Remember that no amount of forcing will help. Each child matures on a personal timeline at their own pace.

Let go of your need to push or force them to advance. Fear not, because Chinese wisdom tells us that "when the student is ready, the teacher appears." And truthfully, they may never be ready to engage with an activity we feel they must do. Perhaps there are other activities that motivate and inspire them and in time, within proper parental guidance, they will find their passion and do what they love. Understand that most kids are always ready for something. They simply need the opportunity to discover what options in life are available. And to be honest, as adults our lives are no different. Even though society tells us it's time to retire at age 65, we may not be ready to do so. Maybe we wish to rewire and refire and not retire. Life is all about timing and desire.

One of the issues with this idea of readiness is how we as parents become frustrated, disappointed, impatient, and confused by what we believe is the failure of our children to give it their all and follow the straight and narrow path of what seems to be the right one but actually is not what they want. You may blame yourself because you or their coach can't seem to motivate them. The truth is, you can inspire and empower these kids, but their motivation comes from within themselves. No one can motivate another person except in a Hollywood movie. All we can do is to provide the safe environment we mentioned before. Kids progress according to their own internal clock, as we said previously, and they will move forward when and if they want to.

In such an environment, much listening is required. Just listen and see what you can learn (see chapter 3 about this topic). Look for an opportunity to fuel their fire, not yours. This will keep their hearts open to you, and when the time is right, they will seek your guidance and advice. They will believe in you and believe that they can be something other than ordinary, regardless of the path they choose.

We must mention that this safe environment requires that it's okay for the child to struggle and even fail. Failure is a teacher and struggle builds resilience and fortitude, enabling them to handle future setbacks and roadblocks on the journey.

Most of all, remember that what we think is best for our child might not be what they believe is best. Let them follow their own hearts and discover what motivates them and what they feel passion for, while in the background, you are an endless supply chain for caring, love, inspiration, and guidance when needed.

Happiness and peace are ours when we refuse to force and make things happen. Yielding conquers pushing; soft is strong.
—Chungliang Al Huang, Tai Ji master and philosopher

Questions on the Quest

1. How do you feel about the concept of readiness as presented here?
2. How does the concept of motivation change how you approach your child and life?
3. What was your favorite takeaway from this discussion and why?
4. What do you need to start doing (that you're not doing) to help with readiness?
5. What do you need to stop doing (that you are doing) to help with readiness?

CHAPTER 7:

GRATITUDE IS AN ATTITUDE

Acknowledging the good that you already have in your life is
the foundation of all abundance.

—Eckhart Tolle, author and visionary

The Navy women's lacrosse team was gathered on the eve of the biggest game of their season, the battle with the Army, their archrival. It's always a make-or-break season event. The pressure on these athletes could be cut with a knife. Head coach Cindy Timchal asked Jerry for a quick Zoom session to align their mental and physical skill sets. The basis of the "Jerry Chat" was the exercise you'll learn about at the end of this chapter, one on full gratitude. When Jerry was finished, he asked the athletes to compete in the game all out, giving back for all they had received in their lives. Each athlete became a servant, giving to their teammates everything they had—whatever it took, even if they had to bleed to do it. This exercise took the focus off the pressure to win and control what they could and compete with heart, a purpose higher and bigger than any victory, and as a result, Navy crushed the Knights and celebrated a 17-11 victory. The real victory was, however, the connection, caring, and love they felt for one another through gratefulness and service.

In Jerry's book *Everyday Champion Wisdom*, he talks about how according to Eastern thought, gratitude is one of the best practices for being the best version of ourselves. It is closely connected to the concept of mindfulness. Practicing gratitude as sports parents helps us to get connected to our lives and see how we are a small part of a larger purpose. It liberates us from worry, endless desires, and the suffering caused by seeing what we lack. Gratitude is the key to personal happiness and joy. It helps us to change fear into faith and faith into courage. It brings about feelings of love, compassion, and connection. It is life-changing. Imagine how an attitude of gratitude could help you to navigate the journey of sports parenting.

Many parents complain about what they or their children don't have—what they're not getting rather than what they have been given. The champion sports parent does not dwell on what they may lack. Rather, the focus is on feeling well, healthy, strong, and all the fortunate opportunities given to them and their children such as friendship, community, growth, development, joy, fun, and being able to be part of the team . . . something bigger than personal gain or loss. It has become well known that gratitude is good for athletics; it stops negativity, rewires your brain, eliminates stress, improves self-esteem, and raises your level of functioning as a parent.

Those who perform at their very best are grateful. They are also happy and joyful, states of mind that translate into being good at what they do. Brother David Steindl-Rast, a Benedictine monk, reminds us that the root of joy is gratefulness. It is not joy that makes us grateful; it is gratitude that makes us joyful.

In the world of sports, parents and their athletes can easily fall into the trap of what's missing: not big enough, strong enough, talented enough, good enough . . . enough already. It's easy to think about scarcity rather than abundance; to be grateful for what we have is more of a challenge. To help with this, I recommend expressing gratitude as a daily practice.

Becoming aware of what is genuinely important and holding that feeling in your heart is important to you, your child, and the life you create. For example, certain items are more constant, as in "I am grateful for my family, my life partner, my ability to make a difference in the lives of others through my work, my healthy body, my comfortable home, my mental clarity, my sense of humor," and so on. Each day, new items get added to the list.

The following is an exercise that has the power to transform you and your child's life and impact everything you do as a champion sports parent:

- Make a list of five or more items that make you feel grateful.
- Go over the list and get connected to how these make you feel: calm, peaceful, loving, fortunate, blessed . . . all feelings of gratefulness. Take in one deep, slow breath through your nose. As you do, take in this feeling of gratitude. Have the feeling surround your heart, then hold your breath for four seconds and slowly release it. Repeat this deep breathing three times.
- Notice how relaxed and peaceful you feel. Now, go about the rest of your day and make everything you do and say a reflection of what you've been given. In other words, give back.

Having gratitude is an attitude that contributes to your overall health and has a profound impact on your sports parenting as you go from "grateful to great."

> Here is a strong, positive affirmation that will direct you to keep on track with the chapter's message.
>
> *I am grateful for all I have been given, and I let my daily life reflect my gratitude for all that I have. Gratefulness is the process of becoming mindful of what is genuinely important and holding that feeling in my heart.*

Look closely and you will find that people are happy because they are grateful.
—Brother David Steindl-Rast

Questions on the Quest

1. What are five things in your life that you are most grateful for?
2. How can you pass the concept of gratitude on to your children?
3. What is the difference between appreciation and gratitude?
4. What can you start doing (that you're not doing) to be more grateful?
5. What can you stop doing (that you are doing) to show more gratitude?

CHAPTER 8:

LET THE RIVER FLOW

I want to make sure that my guys feel valued, respected, important, and relevant. When they do, magic happens, and they compete at higher levels.

—Steve Kerr

Several years ago, when Jerry was serving several sports teams at the University of North Carolina, he approached women's lacrosse head coach Jenny Levy and mentioned how unfortunate it was that he didn't have the chance to meet his idol, men's basketball coach Dean Smith who had retired a few years ago. Brimming with total joy, Jenny announced to Jerry that Coach Smith visited the campus each day to consult with the basketball program. She said excitedly, "Jerry, wow, go make an appointment—he's still on campus!" Jerry was "over the moon" about this opportunity, and covered in sweat, dirt, and torn clothes from practice, he ran down to that office and serendipitously, Coach Smith was there and seemed eager to meet with Jerry.

This first meeting with the iconic basketball coach showed Jerry how brilliant Coach Smith was at the relationship game. He was the kind of leader and parent who, through deep, genuine caring, inspired and empowered Jerry. According to Jerry, "Coach Smith made me feel like I was the most important person in his life, that I mattered, that I was important and relevant." Following this intimate forty-five-minute meeting, Jerry felt so valued and important that he committed himself to writing a new book: *Coaching with Heart*. Jerry often mentions that he would have done anything for this authentic, caring leader.

Like Coach Smith and Coach Kerr, quoted at the beginning of this chapter, you, as a champion sports parent, want to make sure that all children feel *relevant*, *important*, *valued*, *empowered*, and *respected*. These are the feelings that make up the acronym RIVER. We use this touchstone in our coaching and parenting as a reminder of what we need to do and how we must be to give our athletes the opportunity to be loyal, go the distance, work harder, be mentally strong, and feel safe.

Many of the coaches we work with embrace and use the concept of the RIVER. Cindy Timchal, winningest NCAA lacrosse coach of all time, has adopted and adapted the RIVER effect to her coaching style. When she's mindful of using it, she notices that there is a major "buy-in" to her systems. She bathes her athletes in the RIVER and then notices the tsunami of how "the athletes are super willing to put it all out on the field." When you marinate your youngsters in the RIVER, they will respond in a similar fashion.

The substance of water is used widely as a metaphor in Eastern Taoist cultures for guiding, parenting, and leading in a strong and fluid way. We often use it as a way to describe desired motion during athletic events such as basketball, soccer, and lacrosse.

Tao is actually referred to as the Watercourse Way. In fact, it refers to the fluid flow of nature, and this flow of water is often used as a principal metaphor by Lao-Tzu and other Chinese scholars. For a Taoist, water is the basis of all life as it nurtures and nourishes all living things. This is what you do when you use the RIVER as a strategy to parent your child athletes. The RIVER effect becomes the bedrock of a strong connective relationship between you and your children, nurturing them and their friends to thrive and expand in its awesome flow.

The word *RIVER* is not only a wise acronym for focusing on caring for others but also a wonderful metaphor for how to be a champion sports parent. The river is soft yet strong; it wears away rock carving its path along the journey to the ocean as it lights up cities. Yet it is the softest substance you can lay your hands on. Like the river, champion sports parents must be strong and demanding, establish boundaries, set limits, create a path, and yet be kind, respectful, affirming, loving, and caring. Demanding and loving/ soft and strong are, indeed, compatible. And, like the mighty river that gives itself to the land and mother ocean, the greatest sports parents are servants who give to and serve those for whom they are responsible.

Here are a few statements that include the RIVER acronym you can use to win the hearts of your children and the children of others:

- You're important to us and your team. They need your awesome efforts.
- I love your work ethic—it motivates all of us.
- If you keep giving your all, you will be happy and so will your team.
- We value your presence; you bring out the best in everyone.
- That last week of practice was one of your best thus far.
- I want to give you permission to choose the sport that you love.
- When you practice like that, you're being a true champion.
- Without you, your team would not be as good.
- I appreciate and love how much you give of yourself to your teammates.
- Whether you choose sports or not, we still love and value you.

Using the RIVER concept is easy. Simply be aware, catch your kids and others doing something right, and call positive attention to it.

Watch how they feel more significant and become open and ready to go the distance. We believe in and love sports, but what fills our hearts is the unshakable belief that it provides more opportunities for children to feel inspired, empowered, and significant than any other experience in life. Our primary work as champion sports parents is to help these youngsters to feel their significance. Marinate them all in the RIVER.

> Here is a strong, positive affirmation that will direct you to keep on track with the chapter's message.
>
> *When parenting my athletes and others, I make sure I use the RIVER effect each day in a different way. When I do this, I improve the chances of life going well and creating a happy environment for high-level functioning.*

The most important game you will ever win is the relationship game.

—Steve Kerr

Questions on the Quest

1. What are five things in your life that you are most grateful for?
2. How can you pass on the concept of gratitude to your children?
3. What is the difference between appreciation and gratitude?
4. What can you start doing (that you're not doing) to be more grateful?
5. What can you stop doing (that you are doing) to show more gratitude?

CHAPTER 9:

THE PERMANENCE OF IMPERMANENCE

It's not impermanence that makes us suffer. What makes us suffer is wanting things to be permanent when they are not.
—Thich Nhat Hanh, Buddhist monk and author

We told you about Brennan Lynch, Jerry's third son, in the introduction to this book. As you may remember, he was a scholarship athlete at the University of Colorado. His college career didn't last long. One day, he decided he no longer wanted to run for the team, and he dropped out. After guiding him for years in this event, Jerry was disappointed and felt it wasn't the right decision. Such change was difficult to handle. In time, Jerry came to terms with it and realized he needed to follow his own teaching, that all things change for the right reason even if it is not clear at the moment.

Thirteen years later, Jerry now knows it was the best decision his son could have made. There would have been less suffering on Jerry's part had he applied what he knew back when it happened. And like all things in life, while Brennan's running ended in college, now at the age of 33, he has taken up distance running once again and loves it.

There is only one constant in life, and that is that change will happen . . . nothing is permanent but impermanence. The seasons of the year, the weather cycles, the rising of the sun, and setting of the moon all indicate that impermanence is one of life's most important truths. Nothing lasts, and our futile attempts to hold on to things are the genesis of much suffering. Your children will grow up and move on, they will switch teams and sports, and they will have good days and bad days, successful seasons and seasons of struggle.

So it is along your journey of being a champion sports parent. Your children will change and so will their experiences. They'll win; they'll lose. They'll be happy; they'll be sad. Your connection to your child through sports will change. There is nothing to cling to, and if you try to cling, you will be constantly challenged. So, be prepared for change to happen.

The University of Maryland women's lacrosse team won seven consecutive national championships with the help of Jerry's Way of Champions approach. They believed they would not lose. Then it happened . . . several years of not winning the championship. Now, coming full circle, the Terps are back on top. This is very much like the path of the World Champion Boston Celtics who amassed 11 titles in 13 years only to fade a bit in the ensuing years. Recently, they have been back on top and contending for more championships. After many years as the number-one golf athlete in the world, Tiger Woods now struggles to regain his previous form. What goes up must eventually fall.

We must keep this principle in mind when it comes to parenting athletic kids. Sports is a microcosmic classroom for life; it's a moving pendulum, a never-ending process of being recycled. Life as an athlete entails more change than any other experience in life.

Our view on such change is to enjoy when things are up and know that when they turn around, that too will change. Fighting the cycles is futile.

The changes you and your sports child experience will be mostly inner shifts. Their attitudes will change. Their passions will shift. Their interests will wane, and all you can do is listen, observe, suggest, and go with their flow as long as it is safe and healthy.

Needless to say, there will be drastic physical changes as well. What all this demands from us is that we see the big picture about how all things change. Expect it, anticipate it, be flexible, and observe all that goes on . . . or off. Stay awake to the universal rhythms of nature and act in harmony with them rather than fight them. We can't force a round peg into a square hole, right?

Another item on the checklist of change for you as a sports parent is how your child's relationship with you will change at some point. This is what psychologists call the process of individuation. Your child must "leave the nest" in different ways in order to "find themselves," to discover who they really are without you. It is not an easy time for you as a parent, but to be a champion parent, you must let go and, as we say, let God. Your child will come back to you in an even stronger way. Trust this process of change.

Remember that the mythological phoenix consumes itself by fire, and a new bird springs from its ashes, quickly expressing enthusiasm for a new, changed life. And remember, whether you like or don't like the way things are at the moment, they will change.

In the end these things matter most: How well did you love?
How fully did you live? How deeply did you let go?
—Buddhist wisdom

Questions on the Quest

1. What are three things in your life that you hope don't change?
2. What are three things in your life that you hope will change?
3. What can you start doing (that you're not doing) to accept change better?
4. What can you stop doing (that you are doing) to accept change better?

CHAPTER 10:

WIN THE RACE TO THE RIGHT FINISH LINE

Patience is bitter, but its fruit is sweet.

—Jean-Jacques Rousseau, philosopher

Kevin McLaughlin, USA Hockey's former director of Youth Hockey Development, was not looking forward to opening his email in January 2009. He knew it was going to be full of angry posts. He knew he and his colleagues at USA Hockey would be accused of destroying the game and taking the toughness out of the sport. He knew that the haters would be out in full force, trying to run the leaders of USA Hockey's youth development team out the door.

But USA Hockey's leadership also knew they were in the right. They knew that in order to survive, grow, and improve, youth hockey needed to change. They needed kids to play cross-ice hockey in order to get more touches, more interactions, and more enjoyment out of every game.

They knew that body checking was not a necessary component

of 10-year-old hockey, as growing children were more susceptible to injury and less likely to develop skillfully if the game was overly physical.

They knew that there was no need for a 12 and Under national champion to be crowned, as this title served the egos of the adults watching far more than the needs of the children playing.

They knew they needed a new model. Youth sports was on a race to the bottom, and hockey was about to pull out of that race.

They knew they needed to win the race to the right finish line.

The new finish line was focused on enjoyment, development, and increased participation. It worried less about childhood achievement and more about developing lifelong hockey players. They knew that more players who were technically proficient would allow the cream to rise to the top—instead of the current model in many sports of throwing a bunch of eggs against a wall and hoping one doesn't break.

Implementing the best research available, USA Hockey introduced the Athlete Development Model (ADM) in 2009, and today the sport is thriving. In an era when most major youth sports are losing numbers rapidly—since 2010, baseball participation is down 5 percent, basketball is down 8 percent, and soccer is down a whopping 23.5 percent— hockey is growing, setting participant numbers records again in 2016– 2017, and now running programs in all 50 states.

If you are wondering whether this made US Hockey less competitive, look at the stats from 2017. There were four world championship events held, and USA Hockey won all four: Women's World Championship, U20 men, U18 Men, and U18 Women.

John has had the honor of presenting alongside both USA Hockey ADM technical director Ken Martel and Kevin Mclaughlin as they have shared their success story to date, and they both told him how their mantra all these years has been "Let's win the race to the right finish line." USA Hockey's ADM stands out as a model for other sporting organizations trying to fight the decline in youth sports participation numbers, caused in a large part by sports models designed to serve the needs, values, and priorities of adults rather than the children who are participating.[6]

Every national governing body in US sports today is developing their own version of the ADM. They are using science, research, and the best principles from across the globe to reengage kids in sports. It can't happen soon enough!

Every week, we hear horror stories about this race to the bottom in youth sports. We get emails about 8-year-old soccer players being asked to sign contracts stating they will not play another sport during the year. We hear about 10-year-olds who travel long distances to "important tournaments" and then don't get any playing time. We even received an email about a 9-year-old football player whose coach would not even put him in the game during *practice*! When the dad asked the coach why his son didn't play, the response from the coach was, "He doesn't know the plays!" Seriously, coach?

It's time for sensible people to take back youth sports and give it to the kids. It's time to stop focusing on the mad rush to crown the youngest national champion, or rank elementary school kids as the "best 8-year-old baseball team in the US." It's time for the adult agenda to take a back seat to the needs of the kids.

If you are a parent who truly cares about your child's long-term health and well-being, or if you are a coach with the needs of your athletes in mind, I hope you will join us in saying, "It's time to start winning the race to the right finish line."

How do we do this?

---

6 As this great video by USA Hockey demonstrates, if we asked adults to play under the same conditions as the kids, the game is not much fun: https://www.youtube.com/watch?v=cXhxNq59pWg&embeds_referring_euri=https%3A%2F%2F-changingthegameproject.com%2F&feature=emb_imp_woyt.

- **Focus on early engagement, not specialization:** Help your kids fall in love with their chosen sport or sports, and let them own the experience. Engagement is about the love of activity, self-motivated participation, and looking at the short-term ("I love what I am doing") versus the long-term ("Back to the grind"). Sampling different sports early on promotes engagement and increases the likelihood of lifelong participation in sports while decreasing burnout and nonparticipation rates.[7] Kids, even pros, need to "play sports," not work them.

- **Take the long view and win the marathon, not the sprint:** Outside of female gymnastics and figure skating, where athletes peak in their early to mid-teens, in most sports, athletes peak in their 20s. There are many unique pathways to the top, but while pouring a 20-year-old's amount of training hours into an 11-year-old will likely guarantee short-term success, it also sets up many roadblocks for the long-term. If you have a late bloomer, help keep them in the development pathway and foster the love of sport—then watch them learn grit and resilience as they compete against bigger, stronger, faster kids. When they catch up physically, watch out!

- **Focus on behaviors, not outcomes:** Early success in sports is often a result of being bigger, faster, and stronger—or older according to the relative age effect—and not a great predictor of long-term performance. What is a good predictor of excellence in the teenage years and beyond, however, are great behaviors and habits. Is your athlete coachable? Are they a hard worker? Are they committed? Do they listen? Are they accountable? Our job as parents is to help our young athletes form great habits first, and eventually outcomes start to take care of themselves.

---

7   François Gallant, MSc, Jennifer L. O'Loughlin, PhD, Jennifer Brunet, PhD, Catherine M. Sabiston, PhD, Mathieu Bélanger, PhD, "Childhood Sports Participation and Adolescent Sport Profile," December 1, 2017, *Pediatrics*, http://pediatrics.aappublications.org/content/early/2017/11/09/peds.2017-1449.

- **Develop the entire person, not just the athlete:** Sports skills become life skills. No matter how good your kids are at sports, even if they are one of the .01 percent who turn professional, they will still have two-thirds of their life where their life skills matter much more than their sports skills. Sports are a great venue for developing life skills such as working with others, embracing the process, dealing with adversity, and so much more. Be sure that your sporting experience is teaching those things instead of compromising them to win this weekend.

> *Patience, persistence and perspiration make an*
> *unbeatable combination for success.*
>
> —Napoleon Hill

Questions on the Quest

1. What was your biggest takeaway from this chapter?
2. What can you start doing (that you're not doing) to help your child win the right to the right finish line?
3. What can you stop doing (that you are doing) to to help your child win the race to the right finish line?

CHAPTER 11:

EMBRACE THE JOURNEY

Wherever you are right now, let it teach you something. Be kind to yourself on the journey and in the process of who you are becoming.
—Morgan Harper Nichols, author and musician

In his book *The Way of the Champion*, Jerry talks about how the mighty Mississippi River moves slowly at times, only to rapidly speed up in the narrows. Then, as it reverses direction, it appears as though it is off course and returning to the start . . . only to reverse itself again as it heads to its destination, a total of 2,348 miles. If you were in a kayak on the river, you might get nervous and think you were going in the wrong direction. If you embraced and trusted the flow, you would know that it was a temporary setback; you wouldn't get out of the boat and give up on your journey because you trust that if you stay the course, you will arrive at your destination.

The journey of extraordinary sports parenting is like the river. It has many reversals, setbacks, failures, and losses. You will plateau, slow down, stand still, and then speed up and experience the "rapids of growth." All this movement is a natural progression in your evolving process of being an awesome parent for your athletic children.

This is process is no different than what all sports parents experience. We are all in the same boat, so to speak, and this is the point where compassion for one another's journey takes place. Only champion parents acknowledge, trust, and accept this natural process to be so. When you grow daisies, you would never think of pulling them up in order to accelerate their growth as they break through the soil for the first time.

The journey of evolving as a sports parent may be slow. Be patient with consistent effort and give yourself time. There's no need to panic or be fearful. After many years of functioning in the role of sports parents, we are perhaps only halfway there, still experiencing the setbacks and failures, learning from them, and we continue to go forward because we love the ride. It has been an amazing journey of growth, fulfillment, and joy amid the setbacks and failures. To help you with the process, remember the following:

- It's not all about you, but it is about you. You develop, and they follow.

- Stay emotionally engaged with them; love them for being human beings with pure intentions.

- Know the difference between what you can and cannot control. Hint: you can't control your children (or anyone else).

- Detach from results and outcomes and focus on the entire process.

- Be real, be authentic, be genuine, be open, be receptive, and be service-oriented.

We do not pretend to have answers; we simply have some observations. It has been said that there are two ways to obtain wisdom: painlessly from a teacher or painfully from life. Either way works well. We all must learn to be leaders as parents through the ups and downs, like a river. It helps to simply trust and stay the course on these uncharted and turbulent waters of extraordinary sports parenthood.

This process of being a sports parent contains the joy and exhilaration we search for if we are patient and persist through the challenges. Make the effort to be present in this moment with your child. Reliving the past or obsessing about the future is a setup for misery.

> Here is a strong, positive affirmation that will direct you to keep on track with the chapter's message.
>
> *Sports parenting is an up-and-down, ongoing process that unfolds at its own pace. It is an awesome journey of growth, joy, setbacks, victories, and failures. I manage the process well and flow with its direction.*

Trust the process of your life unfolding, and know with certainty,
through the peaks and valleys of your journey, that your soul
rests safe and secure in the arms of God.
— Dan Millman, author of *The Way of the Peaceful Warrior*

Questions on the Quest

1. Why can thinking about the past feel depressing? Why can thinking about the future feel anxious? How does it feel when you stay in present thought patterns about all that is going well?
2. What is your biggest takeaway from the idea of the river?
3. How can the river be applied to your life right now?
4. What do you need to start doing (that you're not doing) to enjoy the process?
5. What do you need to stop doing (that you are doing) to enjoy the process?

PART II:

TEACHING YOUR CHILD THE INNER GAME

The player of the inner game comes to value the art of relaxed concentration above all other skills; he discovers a true basis for self-confidence; and he learns that the secret to winning any game lies in not trying too hard.
— W. Timothy Gallwey

Rick Ankiel was a promising rookie baseball player in 2000, winning 11 games for the St. Louis Cardinals, striking out 194 batters, and finishing second in the National League Rookie of the Year balloting. It was a stellar year by any standards, and due to injuries to other pitchers, he was selected to start Game 1 of the National League Division Series against the Atlanta Braves. Sadly, it all fell apart. After not allowing a run in the first two innings, in the third, Ankiel allowed four runs, walked four batters, and threw five wild pitches before being removed.

In his next start in Game 2 of the National League Championship Series against the New York Mets, he was removed after throwing only 20 pitches. Five of those pitches flew past catcher Eli Marrero. A four batter relief appearance in Game 5 of the series yielded two more walks and two more wild pitches. It had become dangerous to even be in the batter's box against Ankiel.

In 2001, Ankiel began the season with the Cardinals but was soon demoted to Triple A, where in 4.1 innings, he walked 17 batters, threw 12 wild pitches, and had an ERA of 20.77! How can a promising young pitcher, who was the second-best rookie in 2000 and had thrown tens of thousands of pitches in his life fall so far and so fast? Was it technique, or was it something much more important and often overlooked? Was it the inner game?

In Part II: Teaching Your Child the Inner Game, you'll learn how you can better serve your child in the mental aspects of successful performance with less stress, anxiety, fear, tension, and tentativeness. In this section, we share the mental skills and strategies that will help you help your child perform at elevated levels in sports and life with more joy, fun, enthusiasm, passion, and emotional engagement. These are the blueprints we use while working with teams of athletes helping them to achieve their best possible performance. Using these mental skills has helped these athletic teams to win more than 130 championships at the World, National, Conference, State, District, and League levels of competition. You will learn how to pass these proven skills and natural laws on to your child as well as help them to understand how less is more, soft is strong, loss is gain, failure is success, and your opponent is your partner. All of these natural laws will enable you to be a loving, kind, and full human being as your child learns how sports are an awesome preparation for developing vital life skills. When this happens, sport becomes a dynamic activity for physical, mental, emotional, and spiritual development for parents and children alike. The inner game is the North Star, the competitive edge that illuminates the path of sports parenting, performance, and the bigger game of life.

CHAPTER 12:

CHILD AS CHAMPION ATHLETE

You win the game with heart. We spend four years working that muscle.
—Anson Dorrance, head coach, UNC women's soccer

Being a champion is all about competing with heart. In one of Jerry's books, *The Way of the Champion,* he tells the story about the legendary racehorse Seabiscuit, considered by the so-called experts to not have star capability. He lacked all of the traditional earmarks of the truly great traditional champion horses, yet he ran with heart and raced as a champion. Those associated with this legend talk about his demonstrated courage, tenacity, fearlessness, and all the other qualities of champions. He was *being* a champion even before he was crowned one.

Having been an intimate part of more than 130 world, national, conference, and state championship teams as well as more than 1,000 champion athletes, our Way of Champions work knows something about being a champion. Before we clarify how to be a champion, we want to mention that first and foremost, a champion is not something one becomes . . . ever! It is something you are presently *being* by demonstrating the qualities and traits of a champion now. It is a daily commitment to practicing the habits and ways of a champion as outlined in this chapter.

We are not human *doings*; we are human *beings*. We teach you how to teach your child how to *be*, to function in the present moment and embody the process of *being* a champion, which we believe is an intentional, conscious choice, an attitude and a decision that with the right sports parenting, one can make that conscious choice more often.

A champion is one who is present in each moment by being more aware, courageous, patient, happy, caring, connective, selfless, grateful, fearless, loving, competitive, and many other ways of being that are emblematic of exceptional athletes, regardless of age or ability. As such, the champion is not something one does; it is something one either decides to be or not to be. It is part of one's purpose identity, not one's performance identity.

This is the pivotal decision we must all make for ourselves, and as a champion sports parent, you can help your child with that choice. But, when you do, you must make certain that it is a fun, enjoyable, and invigorating process for them. Being a champion is a slow, gradual process of steps going both forward, then backward—but either way, their feet are pointed in the right direction. As a parent, it helps that you provide some guidance by directing and encouraging your children to follow this idea.

Being a champion starts long before any win or result. Being a champion is about building character, belief, trust, and love. Being a champion means facing adversity and growing because of the obstacles encountered along the way. Being a champion means not being afraid of failure, understanding instead that failure is our greatest teacher in life. This concept can be easily absorbed by your youngsters, and it will impact their relationship with all of life. Being a champion means always living according to our standards and values and holding one another accountable along the way. Being a champion means sacrificing individual stats or goals, understanding that we will always go further together. Being a champion is a choice and will never be defined by any result or championship win.

The "champion way" is, in the words of scholar Joseph Campbell, the "hero's journey," an up-and-down, gain-and-loss odyssey of self-discovery. It happens when your children are dedicated to exploring the unlimited boundaries of their full human potential in an environment of caring, connection, and love created by you, the parent. Michael Murphy, in his book *Golf in the Kingdom*, alludes to those of us on such an odyssey as being "astronauts of inner space."[8] Being a champion is an inner journey that has passion, love, and heart. Winning externally on the scoreboard is a by-product of the victories within.

Champions are quick to grasp the difference between what they can and can't control in a sports event. Champion wisdom teaches that outcomes and results cannot be controlled. Preparation, attitude, emotions, work-rate, effort, and doing the "little things" are some elements of competition you can control, and these help you to relax, stay calm, and focus with intent. Pass this notion on to those you parent. When your children know they can control these aspects of their game, it builds confidence, and as we know, a confident, calm attitude helps all of us to perform consistently at higher levels. It's important to realize, though, that even if you control all these aspects of performance, there is no guarantee that the outcome or results will be in your favor. It will, however, enable you to be at your best and feel great satisfaction in the process. This is champion wisdom.

It's important to know that being a champion doesn't always equate to having a medal placed around your neck or hoisting the trophy above your head. It means possessing the specific traits of a champion: courage, tenacity, persistence, fearlessness, and the willingness to suffer and do whatever it takes to succeed. These traits are learned by your children when you, as a champion sports parent, are more aware of

---

8   Michael Murphy, *Golf in the Kingdom* (New York: Penguin Books, 1972), p7.

these strategies and techniques and work at teaching them to your children.

In fact, most champions we have had the honor of guiding never won a medal, trophy, or championship. But they had the right traits to compete like a champion even if they would fail, make mistakes, and have setbacks. Their confidence was rooted in their ability to bounce back after a loss, which enabled them to have an impact on their team as they continued to seek gradual improvement day after day. This confidence is best learned in a safe environment where you teach such an approach.

By competing and living each day like a champion, your children will discover how they can reach extraordinary levels of personal best performance. And, in the process of such performance, they will increase the likelihood of being the best version of themselves as human beings. What we must remember from the opening quote to this chapter is that the making of a champion is all about heart.

Guiding your children to be champions is not about teaching your child "how to," but more about how you can use your life experience and newly accrued wisdom from this book to stimulate, inspire, and empower your precious little athlete to be more aware on the path of what it means to *be* a champion *now*, in this moment as they play, compete, and live with heart.

> *The vision of a champion is bent over, drenched in sweat, at the point of exhaustion, when nobody else is looking.*
> —Anson Dorrance, head coach, UNC women's soccer

Questions on the Quest

1. What is your biggest takeaway from this chapter?
2. In what ways do you now view performance differently?
3. What can you start doing (that you're not doing) to help your child

in this way?

4. What can you stop doing (that you are doing) to help your child in this way?

CHAPTER 13:

THOUGHTS DICTATE DESTINY

Children must be taught how to think, not what to think.
—Margaret Mead

There is a legendary Cherokee story that is emblematic of the greatest battle we'll ever fight—the one between our good and bad thoughts. An old Cherokee grandpa says to his grandson, "A fight is inside me. It's between two wolves. One is evil who has anger, hate, greed, envy, and resentment. The other wolf is good and has joy, love, peace, hope, truth, compassion, and kindness." The grandson thinks about it for a minute, then asks his grandpa, "Which one will win?" The reply is simple: "The one who'll win is the one I feed."

As a champion sports parent, you are in the perfect position to influence the process of how your children think, and this chapter is aligned with that mission. Thoughts can be the cause of much of our kids' suffering, as well as yours as their parents. Science now proves that your thoughts dictate your destiny.

Jerry mentions in his book *Everyday Champion Wisdom* that all of us have between 60,000 and 70,000 thoughts each day. We become defined by these thoughts. Choosing the same thoughts each day leads to the same choices, which leads to the same behavior, which leads to the same experience, which leads to the same emotions. Creating a new performance future is not possible when we do this. Changing these thoughts will create a new road map to a new and more effective performance future. We are shaped by our minds. We become what we think.

We all perform as we think. We all live as we think, and no one other than us can alter our minds. We control our thoughts, and those thoughts control us. The mind is the ultimate cause of our suffering. It is also the source of our happiness. A tamed mind brings happiness; a wild mind brings unhappiness. Changing the suffering mind to the joyful mind is the key to a happy life.

When we are parenting our athletes, we can encourage them to be aware of how thoughts about missing a shot, dropping a pass, losing a race, or striking out feed the possibility of those results happening. Encourage your child to think of how these things could happen, but that this is okay and not the end of the world—there will be other chances. Ask them, as well as yourself, to replace maladaptive thoughts with positive ones, such as:

- "I can do it; I am strong."
- "Next time I'll get it done."
- "I'm an awesome athlete (or parent, or coach)."

A champion sports parent is one who knows that right thinking will lead to freedom from suffering. We all suffer when we worry about outcomes and results. We also suffer when we try to hold on to victory and achievement. I call this negative, uncontrollable process "stinking thinking." Buddhist thought teaches us to let go of our need to not lose. As a parent, ask your children to care more about what they can control, such as their efforts and work ethic, and focus on all the little things, like diving for the 50/50 ball, playing tough defense, communicating on the field, encouraging teammates, and never giving up. This leads to right thoughts, which opens the door to being their very best. It makes it easier to play and compete with less fear, to be present in the moment, and be more tolerant of the ebb and flow of their emotions, their game, their life. Such thought places them in the middle between loss and gain, pleasure and pain, fame and disgrace, praise and blame.

As a champion sports parent, tell your young athletes that their thoughts can strengthen or weaken them. Thoughts have an energy of their own. They even have a strong influence on the healing process when an athlete is injured. Steph Curry of the Golden State Warriors alluded to this concept while nursing his injured leg back to health when he said, "The body feeds off the mind." Basically, this means that if your thoughts about healing are positive, the body will relax itself and allow the blood to flow more easily and rapidly to the injured area as healing begins.

Science proves this to be so by claiming that thoughts are intricately intertwined with our physical selves. Remember that the direction your children's thoughts go is where *they* will go. You can control your thoughts and mitigate your suffering on this planet and in your life, your work, your sport. In the lyrics for his composition "Redemption Song," Bob Marley suggests that we must all work to emancipate ourselves from mental obstructions. If we, as effective parents, don't, who will? When we free ourselves and help our kids to move away from bad thoughts, we create greater peace, calm, confidence, and a stronger outlook in our lives. This inner battle can be won because each of us has the power of choice. Think about how you and your kids may be feeding the bad wolf and replace it with a more positive narrative.

If you want to have fun with your children about the power of thought, ask them to hold one arm straight out to the side, keep it up, and say out loud over and over," I can do it; I am strong." Then gently and slowly apply a bit of downward pressure to push their arm down.

Next, with the same arm, have them try it again but this time have them say," I can't do it; I'm too weak." As you gently push their arm down, notice the vast difference in arm strength when each phrase is recited. This exercise demonstrates how performance follows our thoughts.

Here are some strong, positive affirmations that will direct you to keep on track with the chapter's message.

I practice positive thoughts and experience success as a result.

A champion sports parent is one who knows that right thinking will cause freedom from suffering.

I focus on possibilities rather than disabilities.

The primary cause of unhappiness is never the situation, but your thoughts about it. Be aware of the thoughts you are thinking.
—Eckhart Tolle

Questions on the Quest

1. What thoughts have you recently had that seem to dictate your life?
2. How can you change those thoughts to make you feel better?
3. What can you start doing (that you're not doing) to create positive thoughts?
4. What can you stop doing (that you are doing) to make your thoughts more positive?

CHAPTER 14:

CONFIDENCE IS CONTROLLABLE

It's all about focusing on the controllable little things and preparation that positions you for being confident and ultimate victory.

—Sun-Tzu, *The Art of War*

Carli Lloyd is a US Women's Soccer Team legend, winning two World Cups, two Olympic gold medals, and twice named the FIFA World Player of the Year. In her long and storied career, she made more than 300 international appearances for the United States and even scored a hat trick in the 2015 World Cup Final. You would think that a player with her ability and experience would be confident, and you would be right. But that confidence was earned.

"I'm not a superstitious person," says Lloyd. "Your preparation is what prepares you, what instills confidence." And no one prepared like Lloyd. She was meticulous in her training, putting in the hours technically, in the film room, and in the weight room. She was always fit, always strong, and always left it all out on the training pitch. Why was Lloyd so confident? Because she always stepped on the field knowing that she had outworked her opponent that day. Why was she able to score a hat trick in a World Cup Final? "Those 16 minutes [in the 2015 World Cup final] were really 13 years of training that no one saw."

It has been said that your opponent's greatest advantage is your lack of confidence in yourself. Developing personal confidence on a regular basis is your greatest competitive advantage. Let us explain how this concept has worked with athletes from the high school level up to world champions at the professional level so you can help your child maximize the percentage of time they spend competing with confidence.

Performance pressure and anxiety impact all levels of competition. There is an obsession in our society about performance outcomes (performance identity) rather than purpose (purpose identity). When overly concerned about outcomes and results, you get mentally bogged down, and it undermines your confidence.

For example, when an athlete shows up to win the game, they get tight, tense, tentative, stressed, and anxious because they know the outcome can't be controlled. When such nervous and fearful feelings occur, self-doubt sets in and confidence wanes. The loss of confidence creates undesirable levels of performance.

On the other hand, when athletes show up to compete and focus only on the little things they can control rather than the outcome and results, they play relaxed, calm, and focused—and confidence rises with the subsequent improvement of performance.

An example of the little things you can control in basketball would be to concentrate on boxing out, crashing the boards, sprinting the lanes, diving for the 50/50 ball, and playing tough, never giving up defense. When these five are executed brilliantly, confidence climbs and performance is at a higher level.

We recommend that you explain this to your children. Some may not be ready for this, but we have observed kids 12 and older who really understand and feel a sense of freedom when they do not have to make results happen, which is impossible anyway. When the time arrives to compete, encourage those who do get it to focus only on what can be controlled—the little things they and their coach agree are the essential elements for competition. Later in this book, we talk about how to approach a coach and make suggestions that could enhance your athlete's performance. When coaches get on board with this concept, the sports culture with the team improves drastically in a safer, less pressurized environment.

The key to having confidence more often for all of us at all levels of sport is to silence the expectation factor about performance-based results and emphasize a more process-driven, purpose-driven approach—a more controllable approach of focusing only on the little things, those controllables determined by the coaches and athletes. We have worked with several high schools this past year who used this purpose-driven, Way of Champions approach to win conference and state titles feeling confident throughout. They possessed a tremendous advantage over their opponents whom on paper couldn't be defeated but were. The WOC teams and athletes focused on the joy and fun of playing and controlled the little things. Perhaps the best statement we can make is this: You may or may not win the game, but by using this approach, you will position yourself for your best possible performance.

Here are a few strong, positive affirmations that will direct you to keep on track with the chapter's message.

Every day, in every way, I let go of outcomes and focus on efforts to control what I can and watch my confidence surge.

I think about what I can control and what I can't and have the wisdom to know the difference.

If I am not confident, it is probably because I focus on the outcome and results.

You will never have confidence in the attainment of an outcome or result. You can't control those and that lack of control leads to a loss of confidence. To gain confidence, you must focus only on what you can control, and all your fear and anxiety will blow away in the wind.
—Jerry Lynch, PhD

Questions on the Quest

1. What have you learned in this chapter that could have an immediate impact on your life?
2. How could this approach help in other contexts beyond sports, such as a job interview or talking in front of a large group?
3. What can you start doing (that you're not doing) to help improve your child's confidence?
4. What can you stop doing (that you are doing) to help improve your child's confidence?

CHAPTER 15:

WHEN LOSING IS WINNING

Every arrow that hits the bullseye is the result of a hundred misses.
—Buddhist saying

It was the year 2013. Jerry was helping the University of North Carolina women's lacrosse team. They had just lost their second straight game to their ACC (Atlantic Coast Conference) rivals and perennial national champions, the University of Maryland. Following the loss, the UNC locker room was filled with tears and heads hanging down to the floor.

The next day, at a team meeting prior to practice, their coach shocked them with the question: "Why are we a better team because of that setback last night?" The athletes' focus was now surprisingly shifted from the pain of defeat to the advantages of losing and how loss makes us better. They came up with seven ways their failure taught them to become a better team.

As life would have it, four weeks later, these two powerhouses met once again in the national championship game. UNC battled every minute into the third overtime period, when they scored the winning goal to capture their very first national championship. Their prior defeats were actually their best teachers that, when noticed, helped them learn and be a better team because of those failures.

Whenever you miss the target, make a mistake, lose, and fail, you are getting closer to knowing how to succeed. Failure is an indication that the teacher has arrived and the lessons can be learned. As an example, Jerry's flagship bestselling book was rejected for publication thirteen times. Every time a publisher said no, Jerry learned what was missing that would make it a better book.

Thinking Body, Dancing Mind has had a 33-plus-year run in 10 languages and still sells well. The ancient book of Chinese wisdom, the *Tao Te Ching*, written more than 2,000 years ago, claimed that we lose yet in this way win.

Champions understand that failure is a necessary and inevitable prerequisite to their ultimate victories. Your children, like you, will learn more from their setbacks than their successes. It is up to you and their coach to consistently redirect your kids toward this way of thinking. As a result, your children will experience less fear, anxiety, and stress, allowing them to be more relaxed, calm, and paradoxically, perform at higher levels.

Whenever your children experience a loss, setback, mistake, or failure, wait a day and then ask, "Why are you a better athlete now than you were before that loss?" By doing this, you train your children to see the connection between their lackluster performance and how it helps them improve. This message, once adapted, will serve them well in the bigger game of life.

Another idea you can use to help kids learn from prior performances is to ask them this series of questions after they compete. First—and it must be first—"What went well?" This gets them to focus on the good they did at a time when their focus is on the negative. Next ask, "What needs work?" This is a more proactive approach than the familiar, more reactive question, "What went wrong?" These two questions open a child's heart to possibility rather than inability. They begin to see how loss and failure, although disappointing, are not as crippling as they originally seemed. This makes setbacks more tolerable and at times, more important. How amazing it is to embrace failure as an extraordinary path of growing mentally and emotionally and as an opportunity to develop the inner strength to develop one's full human capacity!

With this wise guidance, your child will begin to understand that great athletes like Kobe Bryant, Michael Jordan, Simone Biles, and others all admit that their failures were their greatest mentors and teachers. They all made it a habit to take what they learned in defeat and turn it into a gift for achieving higher levels of competitiveness in the future.

> Perhaps a good affirmation to pass on to your children that will help them embrace this concept is:
>
> *All my mistakes, setbacks, and failures are my best teachers that help me to get better and better every day.*

Failure is the condiment that gives success its flavor.
—Truman Capote

Questions on the Quest

1. How can you apply this concept to your personal life each day?
2. What have you learned from this chapter that makes your life easier and fluid?
3. What failure experiences in your past have helped to make you who you are today?
4. What can you start doing (that you're not doing) to learn from loss?
5. What can you stop doing (that you are doing) to allow loss to be your teacher?

CHAPTER 16:

GO SLOWER, ARRIVE SOONER

Patience is a virtue . . . . When you're younger you're very impatient. You want things to happen right away overnight, which is not possible."
—Novak Djokovic, world champion professional tennis athlete

True story: An athlete went to her coach and asked how long it would take to develop into a world-class triathlete. He reassured her that if she trained slowly and diligently, it would take four to five years to reach that level. Feeling frustrated and impatient with his answer, she told him she didn't want to wait that long; she wanted to be there sooner. She then asked, "How long will it take if I work harder, faster, and with more effort?" His response: "Ten to twelve years." Working harder is a setup for fatigue, injury, and burnout, leading to a delay in the progress.

By now, you probably have discovered the truth behind Djokovic's statement about a lack of patience in youngsters. They all want to be champions without slowing down to put the time and effort into such an accomplishment. Let us share our perspective about patience, one that will benefit your children—and hopefully you, too, because we all struggle with this concept.

Patience, as we define it, is the ability to slow down, enjoy, and immerse yourself in the process—the flow of life as it assumes its own form and shape. This is an important virtue for athletes to master. Most young stars want success, and they want it now. They want to play more, earn more, get more, and do so sooner than later. Such a focus makes all of these aspiring athletes tight, tense, and stressed, which in turn delays their hopes and dreams.

Unfortunately, this story is all too common. We experience this in our work with not just the younger athletes but also those at the professional level. Our best advice to you and your children is to adopt the Japanese concept of Kaizen, the slow, gradual, incremental process of continual improvement on the path of mastery. We suggest using the mantra "Go slower; arrive sooner."

Remember that in life and therefore in sports as well, things happen not when you think they should, but when they are supposed to, when the time is right. Everything happens for a good reason. When one surrenders, lets go, and gives up the struggle to make something happen, things occur at the very best time. Have you noticed this in your life?

Children have a tendency to push, force, and shove . . . and so do many of us adults. But regardless, life has its own plan. As previously mentioned, rushing leads to injury, pushing leads to burnout, and forcing leads to failure. Nature offers all of us an opportunity to get better without knowing it: the plateau. It is that sacred space in which not moving forward is the chance to master what we've already learned, to get better before we leap forward to the next level. In fact, we all experience the plateau before going to the next level. The problem is our impatience with what we see as standing still when it is really a time of improving what has already been learned. The plateau is a necessary and inevitable stage on the path of excellence.

As a champion sports parent, you can reassure your children that it's okay to have this time to improve—that with patience, persistence, and consistent good work, the rewards will follow. Of course, know that they watch how you behave—are you patient and tolerant of your own plateaus?

Refuse to let your children or yourself get caught in society's pressure trap of rapid achievement. Not now does not mean never. Tell your child that with patience, the best will happen and not expect to constantly go forward. When everyone has fun and enjoys nature's process, all will advance sooner than later. The laws of nature point out that if we are patient, everything comes at the right moment and when we are most ready.

You have to find this balance between urgency and patience. You've got to work urgently, but you have to remain patient.
— Steve Kerr

Questions on the Quest

1. What do you notice happens when you impatiently want to achieve something?
2. When you have been patient about something in the past, how did things go?
3. What can you start doing (that you're not doing) to help your child be patient?
4. What can you stop doing (that you are doing) to foster patience in your child?

CHAPTER 17:

FROM VISUALIZATION
TO REALIZATION

*If your mind is empty, it is always ready for anything; it is open
to everything. In the beginner's mind there are many
possibilities; in the expert's mind there are few.*
—Shunryū Suzuki, author of *Zen Mind, Beginner's Mind*

Many of the best athletes in the world embrace visualization as a way
to be mentally focused and emotionally present. This has been happening at all levels of performance for many years. Even Michael Jordan,
following his winning shot against the Utah Jazz in 1997 for one of his
NBA championships, ran over to the bench and loudly commented to
his teammates about his visualization practice: "This stuff really works!"

Ryan Bernacchi, a retired US Navy captain, Top Gun instructor,
and former commander of the Blue Angels, knows something about
visualization. Ryan recently was a guest on our *Way of Champions
Podcast*, where he talked extensively about teamwork and culture. One
of the essential tools for his teams was how he and his crew would

simulate every flight using the skill of mindful visualization. He called it "flying in a chair."

The night before a mission or a Blue Angels air show, he would sit in a chair and close his eyes and imagine the entire flight ahead. He would make all the calls as lead pilot, out loud, and visualize by feeling every takeoff, maneuver, and landing. He would then repeat it over and over until he had seen and felt the entire mission before he did it in real time. He mentioned how all great pilots fly every flight in their heads before flying the actual mission by emptying their minds of the daily chatter, then filling them with the mission at hand. It was in this quiet time that his confidence was gained and his inner voice said, "I'm ready!" This is how his squadron became trustful, connected, caring teammates. You can do this as well.

Similarly, Coach Phil Jackson was the master of using visualization and meditation with the Chicago Bulls and Los Angeles Lakers on his way to winning 11 championship rings. In Jackson's book *Eleven Rings*, he devotes several detailed pages on his thoughts about Suzuki's *Zen Mind, Beginners Mind* approach to his team's performance.[9] To help players on both teams become better teammates, quiet the chatter of their minds, and focus on the nature of the inner game, he introduced the athletes to the concept of mindful visualization.

Simply defined, mindful visualization or meditation means to be aware and pay attention to the present moment with intention. It's about focusing on what is happening right now. Phil would get the players to sit in a room for 10 minutes to help them become more connected and focused teammates. He called it "the warrior room."

All the athletes who took part in this voluntary exercise loved it. It was a special, unified group who were, in the words of Vietnamese teacher Thich Nhat Hanh, "dwelling happily in the present moment," with quiet, simple, clear minds. Phil Jackson found through such practice that when his athletes marinated themselves fully in the inner game, they developed

---

9 Phil Jackson, *Eleven Rings: The Soul of Success* (New York: Penguin Books, 2014).

a deeper, stronger awareness of one another, and they fully focused on the present moment of the basketball game and on being a great teammate.

One of Jackson's protégés, Golden State Warriors head coach Steve Kerr, knows something about championships as well and has chosen mindfulness as one of the team's core values. In conversations with Steve, we've talked about the importance of mindful meditation and visualization to help him with his leadership and help his players be great teammates. We tell you all this in hopes that you will consider visualization and meditation as a skill to teach your child to learn how to strengthen their inner game for higher performance levels.

There is an ancient proverb that states, "If you know the art of breathing you have the strength of ten tigers." Over the years, Jerry has trained thousands of coaches and athletes to have tiger strength using a 2,500-year-old form of Buddhist meditation called *Vipassana*, a Pali word that when translated means "insight." This inner game of visualization meditation practice relies on the awareness that breathing is happening and using the breath as a focal point to quiet what Buddhists call the "monkey mind." Jerry calls this process "feelingization" because it is imperative that one "feels" what is happening, "feels" the behaviors and actions that you'd like to replicate during an event.

This meditative state of mind, this "still point," is a sacred space that raises awareness and makes movement effortless and confidence more robust. It helps us to find balance and keep it in our lives. It is a source of positive energy and helps us to remain connected with our team in a positive way. It has a direct, powerful influence on your child and the team's performance.

It is interesting to notice how animals instinctively know and use a method of stillness in nature. They all meditate. Observe the heron poised motionless on one leg, the monkey climbing to the uppermost branch, the snake basking in the warmth of the summer sun, or the cat lying on a pillow, eyes focused on a small object. Such stillness prepares the inner environment for a deep, peaceful, meditative state.

Being mindful will help your children to win the inner game and become a better version of themselves. Mindfulness visualization has actually become profoundly relevant in mainstream America, being embraced by hospitals helping patients to heal, military groups wanting to focus, educational systems hoping to facilitate learning, musicians wishing to be more present, actors trying to stay in the moment, and countless elite athletes working to maximize their performance. It will even help you, the parent, to feel what it is like to be the best parent you can be.

This is a learned strategy that can strengthen your wishes to become more inspired, more self-aware, and a better athlete and parent. There is no better venue for practicing meditation than athletics. The benefits are realized almost immediately.

If you're ready to learn this skill so you can teach it to your children, begin this inner game with eyes closed, in a quiet place, free from interference. Sit comfortably in a chair with your back straight and your feet on the floor. Drop your arms into your lap, and take the following 5 steps:

1. Begin by taking three deep, controlled breaths, holding the oxygen in your lungs with each breath for three seconds before you exhale. Notice how this procedure has an instant effect on your body and mind, relaxing you immediately. Then stop and return to normal breathing.

2. Simply notice that breathing is happening. Watch your breath come in and go out. Do not control its natural flow other than to have it go through the nostrils.

3. When your mind wanders—and it will—simply acknowledge it and direct it back by saying, "Wandering, come back." Don't be concerned about wandering; it's natural. In fact, the act of being aware of the wandering and bringing your attention back to the breath actually helps you to develop strong attention skills when you are competing in everyday life. It develops what we call

"meta-attention." Wandering is an integral aspect to the full meditation/feelingization practice.

4. Do this "breath watching" for five to eight minutes, then switch gears and begin to visualize by *feeling* yourself being how you wish to be as the champion sports parent bringing out the best in your children. Visualize for about four minutes.

5. Following your "feelingization," recite a few short, positive affirmations that nurture and support your feelings. Unlike visualizations which involve how you feel and what you see, these strong statements influence what you say and, more importantly, how you think. Thoughts strengthen or weaken you and determine the direction in which you go. Affirmations are spiritual gems that keep you on the path to parent with heart. Write them out on index cards, and as you recite them, feel the words as if they are real and happening now.

If the spirit of many in body but one in mind prevails among the people, they will achieve all their goals, whereas if one in body but different in mind, they achieve nothing remarkable.
—Nichiren, 13th century Japanese Buddhist teacher

Questions on the Quest

1. What can you do to help yourself use this skill each day for 5 to 20 minutes?
2. What are your takeaways from this chapter that will impact your life?
3. How could you introduce this skill set into the life of your child?
4. How can you use visualization in your life to realize more possibilities?
5. What can you start doing (that you're not doing) to develop the skill of visualization—with children or in your own life?
6. What can you stop doing (that you are doing) to develop the skill of visualization—with children or in your own life?

CHAPTER 18:

BEING A GIVER, NOT A GETTER

One player with a selfish attitude can poison a locker room and make it hard, if not impossible to establish teamwork. Sport is about unselfish acts.
—Dean Smith, iconic Hall of Fame basketball coach at Carolina

One of the stories we love to tell our teams is the one about Andre Iguodala of the Golden State Warriors. When Steve Kerr took over as head coach with the Warrior organization, one of his first acts was to talk with Andre about his role on the team. Andre, an NBA All-Star, was a consistent starter on every team he played for, every game of his career. Kerr asked him how he'd feel if he didn't start with the Warriors but instead come off the bench when needed. Kerr told him how that would make the team better. Andre unselfishly responded that he would agree to do whatever is best for the team. He trusted Kerr, and he gave to his team in this way all season. Andre was called upon to start in the finals of the championship series, and his stellar performances earned him the MVP of the 2015 NBA Finals. The Warriors won their first championship with Steve Kerr, and all this happened because Andre chose to selflessly win the day. He so embraced his selfless role that when he published his autobiography, he titled it *The 6th Man.*

Because of the high priority Steve Kerr puts on selflessness, his players find joy in giving to one another. When you as a parent place a high priority on being selfless, your children will learn the value of giving and how that feels. Steve says that the concept of selflessness is counterintuitive in professional sports where many worry about getting enough—money, playing time, statistics, recognition—yet he has found a way to create a giving culture. His method is to ask players to be mindful of giving to one another as a way to ultimately get more in return. Notice how unselfishly they distribute the ball, throw an extra pass, and give credit to others for their contribution.

Perhaps it is a generational thing, but it appears as though the question most athletes ask these days is "What can I get?" rather than "What can I give?" They seem more concerned about how many minutes they will play, how much money they can make, how big a scholarship they can get, and how many points, goals, or hits they can make. At all levels—from PeeWee to Pro—it seems to be a culture that cares more about themselves as individuals than the team at large. As a champion sports parent, you can raise the mental strength of your children in athletics by teaching them about the virtue of selflessness.

Bill Bradley, senator, author, and all-American and professional basketball national champion with the New York Knicks, comments, "The greatness of my teams is how they realized that no one player could be as good as all of the players competing together unselfishly."

This chapter's opening quote was part of a conversation Jerry and Dean Smith had while Jerry was working at UNC. It was Coach Smith who promoted the "pointing finger," a gesture made by pointing to the teammate who assisted you on scoring a basket as a way to share the effort. This was part of what he called "The Carolina Way," a way of caring and connecting unselfishly and giving to others.

This isn't easy in today's world. Many coaches struggle with getting athletes to "buy in" to the notion of giving rather than getting. As a parent, you need to consider being more demanding of your children about this core value and teach them how to embrace it more fully. They need to know that sustained selflessness becomes its own reward. When we give to others, others give back exponentially, and this helps everyone to win the day.

In Anson Dorrance's soccer culture at the University of North Carolina, the athletes learn to put the team before themselves. Mia Hamm, a member of their championship teams, talks about the champion being the team, not any one individual player. We've observed Anson's teams in practice and truthfully, they are a clan of generous people who place teams above self.

Nancy Stevens, former head coach of the UConn Husky women's field hockey national champions, shared her take on the value of selflessness with Jerry while he was working with her team. She started by quoting an African Proverb: "If you want to go fast, go alone. If you want to go far, go together." She went on to say:

> During the recruiting process, we often identify players who are supremely talented but simply won't fit into our team culture. There is only one ball on the field! We look for players who enjoy sharing the ball. If you give up the ball, you will always get it back. The synergy created by playing as a team will often succeed against teams that depend on one of two superstar players. This philosophy has allowed us to win three of the past five NCAA National Championships.

> On a more personal note, I have had the good fortune to travel extensively in Africa over the past decade. Observing the strength of the tribe has inspired me to

share aspects of those strong cultures with our team. I have also learned a great deal from observing herds of elephants. Dame Daphne Sheldrick, who founded the Sheldrick Trust to rescue orphan elephants, has said many times that "elephants possess all the best qualities of human beings and very few of the worst." I have observed the herd waiting for and protecting a younger elephant that limped slowly with a twisted leg. It was a congenital defect that prevented the younger elephant from keeping up with the herd. Rather than abandon the family member, different herd members took turns walking alongside this slower elephant. That is just one example of many that can be learned on the Masai Mara.

As far as implementing selflessness goes, you may want to try one of our favorite exercises with your children (and their team, assuming their coach would be into it). To get teams to think more selflessly, we ask everyone to choose one way they will give to the team that week, picking from a list of 10 items drawn up by the entire team. They send a "group text" informing their teammates about their generosity for the week, and they keep one another accountable for doing the work. Younger athletes who don't text can tell their teammates in a short meeting before practice. It might be picking up all the balls after practice, carrying the ball bag, giving more praise to others, or volunteering to help other teammates with skill development. After a few weeks, the team begins to feel the shift, and this creates a stronger bond between the players. The connection deepens and the caring blossoms. The athletes become givers rather than getters.

According to the Dalai Lama: "Our prime purpose in this life is to give to and help others." Russian novelist Leo Tolstoy also claimed that our sole meaning in this life is to serve humanity.

There is a beautiful and compelling story about selflessness told by Native American Lakota historian Joseph Marshall III. He refers to selflessness as generosity.

> Early in the 19th century, a group of Lakota moving camp were forced to wait for an entire day while a herd of buffalo, numbering in the hundreds of thousands, passed by. A young boy sat, somewhat impatiently, with his grandmother as they watched. "Why are there so many?" he asked. The old woman smiled lovingly and replied, "Because there is no end to the Earth's generosity. Do not let there be an end to yours."

Nothing can give you greater joy than doing something for another.
—John Wooden, UCLA basketball coach

Questions on the Quest

1. What is your major takeaway from this chapter?
2. How can you model selflessness with your child?
3. In what ways do you give to others daily?
4. What can you start doing (that you're not doing) to teach your child about giving?
5. What can you stop doing (that you are doing) to teach your child about giving?

CHAPTER 19:

EXCELLENCE, NOT PERFECTION

Perfection belongs to the gods. The most we can hope for is excellence.
—Carl Jung, psychologist

While working with the Boston University women's field hockey team several years ago, Jerry remembers how a very talented athlete, one of the best on the team, was struggling to regain her confidence. If it wasn't a perfect performance, she would be devastated and sulk for hours, if not days. At the request of the coach, Jerry met with this athlete, and the first thing he said to her was: "What's the most important thing right now that we should talk about?" She immediately responded, with no hesitation, "My dad."

It turned out that he withheld his love from her when she didn't perform perfectly. In fact, he told her that he would stop coming to the games unless her performance improved. This was heartbreaking for her as she wanted to be loved, so she felt more pressure to achieve and be perfect. Joy, fun, and excitement were missing. Her father's love was conditional.

Following several individual sessions with her, she began to embrace the idea of excellence rather than perfection. Jerry initiated a conversation with her dad and explained the ramifications of his hurtful behavior. To his credit, he was open and receptive to this new approach, realizing how his behaviors shut his daughter down. Not every story has such a happy ending, but he changed in time to experience his daughter recover from his hurtful ways. She came back to lead the team, and he got to see her excel without perfection.

We have worked with thousands of athletes between the ages of 6 and 36. We notice two distinct truths about this group of strivers:

1. They all fall into one of two categories: those who fail and those who will. It's called the law of human behavior—the inevitability for things to come and go. You're up, then you're down; you win, then you lose. These are natural cycles in all of life. Because of this, perfection is unattainable.
2. More than half these kids suffer from what we call "perfection attention," the act of constantly being obsessed with being perfect and measuring self-worth by outcomes and results that cannot be controlled.

What we do know about the state of perfection is that science has proven it is unattainable. As the opening quote states, perfection belongs to the gods while excellence, the process of doing your very best in the moment, is something we can all achieve.

Having the unattainable goal of being perfect positions us for failure. The effort involved in working toward something that is impossible to achieve causes stress, tension, anxiety, and pressure, all of which detract and inhibit our best personal performances. We have noticed that many parents play a significant role in this malady because they unintentionally and unconsciously believe that they are better parents if their kids are perfect. Because of this, kids feel disappointed in themselves, and they are frustrated and upset about not measuring up to such high, impossible standards.

If perfection were possible, then why is a shot missed at the buzzer in basketball? Why do we have triple bogies? Why do the best hitters in the game fail to hit above .400? Why can't gymnastic athletes score a 10 all the time? Top PGA athletes repeatedly miss putts within 4 feet of the cup. NFL receivers drop the ball in the end zone as time runs out. All athletes fail, commit errors, and lose. They all commit to doing their best they can, and this positions them for personal and team best performances, but they are never perfect. Everyone is perfectly imperfect; imperfection is the only thing we can be perfect at.

While no one can achieve perfection, the idea is still useful as a beacon, a standard to keep us on the path of what is called excellence. To help our children with this debilitating goal, we can show them the ways we are not perfect but still strive to be our very best. We need to be vulnerable and shatter the illusion that they may have about how perfect we are.

Share your imperfections, your failures, your mistakes, and your rejections. While we think the writing of this chapter needs to be perfect, we realize that's not possible. Instead we continue to reread it, make corrections, and settle upon a finished product that is excellent, a chapter that accomplishes our mission. We refuse to measure our worth as authors by how good it is. Our message to everyone is: "Hey, we're not perfect, and we are still really good enough to write this book."

As a sports parent, take the time to notice the ways you emphasize external achievement, care about others' opinions, fear failure, dwell on negative outcomes, and engage in criticism. When you act this way, your children receive the unspoken message that they too must be perfect.

Finally, and most importantly, be aware of the possibility of unintentionally withholding your love when your children do not live up to their given talents. We have observed many parents who make their love conditional upon performance. Because your children crave being loved, they begin to feel pressure to achieve and be perfect. You may want them to feel joy, excitement, and the pleasure of high-level performance, but the message becomes obscured by those who interpret it as needing to be perfect. In our work, we have observed such situations hundreds of times.

All of this is to say that by being less rigid about results and outcomes, you will reduce your children's anxiety and fear, and as a result, their performances will be more aligned with what seems to be excellent. The focus for you as a parent and your child as an athlete is simple: Do your best today to be the best you can be to position yourself for excellent performance.

Here are two affirmations to help you prioritize excellence over perfection:

Perfection is for the gods. My children and I strive, instead, for excellence which means doing all the little things as best as we can and not measure ourselves by outcomes and results.

Performance can never be perfect. Trying to achieve it is a waste of time. Instead, I aspire to be excellent and be "perfectly imperfect."

There is only one goal: to do your best today in order to be the best you can be at this moment. In this way, you position yourself for an excellent, not perfect, performance.
—Sun-Tzu, *The Art of War*

Questions on the Quest

1. When do you get down on yourself—and why?
2. How do you address the perfection trap in your life?

3. What takeaway from this chapter will help you and your child focus on excellence rather than perfection?
4. What can you start doing (that you're not doing) to help your child with perfection attention?
5. What can you stop doing (that you are doing) to help your child with perfection attention?

CHAPTER 20:

BEACONS ILLUMINATING THE WAY

Success is a journey, not a destination.
The doing is often more important than the outcome.
—Arthur Ashe, world champion tennis athlete

Years ago Jerry worked with an Olympic athlete who was one of the top three in her sport in the country. Only two athletes would make the team at the Olympic trials. This added pressure was enough to convince her she needed help and that led her to seek Jerry's service for this matter. She told Jerry that her goals added pressure that exacerbated her tension and anxiety, but it would be a huge disappointment if she failed to reach those goals.

Here is how Jerry helped her to get past the tension and make the Olympic team. He told her that goals are like beacons, flashing lights on the horizon that guide us to stay on track during a satisfying and rewarding journey. They shine in the distance, encouraging movement toward the extraordinary.

In his book *Everyday Champion Wisdom*, Jerry makes the point that for many young athletes, goals become the end, the reason to be in sports.

This creates enormous anxiety and pressure, which makes goal achievement less attainable. But often this is because we, as parents, send the incorrect message that the objective is to attain the goal rather than focus on what that goal provides—an exciting, fun-filled journey. We encourage you to use this new way of talking about goal setting with your children as well. For many of your children (or athletes at any level), setting goals in the traditional way creates tension, anxiety, and pressure as focus shifts from the process to outcomes and results. We invite you instead to encourage your children to set lofty goals and dream about their realization, and then pull back and enjoy being in the moment and involved in doing all the little things that are necessary to keep them on target. If they should fall short, tell them they will still have achieved more than if their focus had been shortsighted. We like to say, "If you shoot for the moon and fall short, you'll still be with the stars."

The most crucial key to success with goals is to help your kids not measure their self-worth by any outcome. Let the goals function as that distant lighthouse, guiding them from afar to move and perform in the present moment, one day at a time, and see how close they can get to fulfilling them.

Teach them to set goals in the spirit of passion, aligning the goals with what they love and then enjoying their movement and progress toward the lantern they have set to illuminate their way. For the potter, the treasure is not found in the finished pot but in the experience of making it. For the marathoner, the real prize is not the completion of the race but the dynamic three months of training that precede it.

In the ancient art of archery, the archer focuses on the true bull's-eye—the Dantien, or gut center, of this physical and emotional being—as they release the arrow. If they are truly centered and their goal is to be the best they can be (the real target), they will experience success no matter where the arrow lands. The real target is within, and the achievement of the external goal is a mere reflection of them hitting this inner bull's-eye.

See if you can help your child to embrace goals this way. For many of us, it seems counterintuitive, but when you think about it, so is much of what we are sharing in this book. The champion athletes we work with embrace this out–of–the–box approach daily, and their joy and excellent performance are testimonies to the validity of this way of approaching goal setting. As a sports parent, encourage your children to stretch and think big, yet at the same time be realistic and know that the stretch is not necessarily a place to get to, but rather a destination that will bring them further than without that stretch. Celebrate the fun and excitement of the journey, the process of being the best you can be.

> Here are some affirmations you can apply to your own exciting life so you can show your children how it works for you.
>
> *I use all my goals as simple guides that keep my feet pointed in the right direction on the path of mastery.*
>
> *Goals are like beacons, flashing lights on the horizon, that guide me to stay on track during a satisfying and rewarding journey.*

It is good to have an end to journey toward,
but it is the journey that matters in the end.
—Ernest Hemingway

Questions on the Quest

1. In retrospect, what goals did you set in the past that you did not achieve? How did that feel?
2. How can the concepts in this chapter make it easier for you to set good goals?

3. What are some goals you feel you can set now?
4. What can you start doing (that you're not doing) to help your kids set goals they are willing to try?
5. What must you stop doing (that you are doing) help your kids set goals they are willing to try?

CHAPTER 21:

COURAGE TO GIVE YOUR ALL

There's no comparison between what's lost by not trying
and what's lost by not succeeding.

—Francis Bacon, philosopher and statesman

Ronda Rousey was the first American woman to win an Olympic judo medal, a bronze in the 2008 games. She parlayed that into an extremely successful mixed martial arts career, becoming a champion and setting a record by defending her title six times. In 2018, she became the first woman inducted into the UFC Hall of Fame, and she has since moved into professional wrestling. You would think that an athlete who was the best fighter in the world was fearless, but that is not the case.

"People say to me all the time, 'You have NO fear,'" said Rousey. "I tell them, 'No, that's not true. I'm scared quite a bit. Because of that fear, I get the chance to demonstrate my courage. I'm a courageous person who has fear, but I go ahead anyway.'" Truth be known, the difference between someone without courage and someone with courage is this. Those without courage have a lot of fear. Those with courage have a lot of fear . . . but they go ahead anyway and take the risk to improve their circumstances.

In the words of author Ray Bradbury about risk-taking: "First you jump off the cliff and build your wings on the way down." It takes courage amid the intense fear to jump and trust that you'll build your wings and be fine. Most people stand at the top waiting endlessly for the wings to be built before they jump. We're talking about the courage to take that plunge—a risk few are willing to take. It's like the story of the young boy in Paulo Coelho's *The Alchemist* who takes the trek across a vast desert trusting that there will be a caravan coming in his direction that will have the supplies he needs to complete the journey. And, before long, he sees the caravan slowly moving toward him.

Life is filled with stories of heroes, risk-takers, and warriors of indomitable spirit who take the chance they are given to realize something greater than they can imagine. This is what a champion parent or athlete is all about. It's about having the courage to act and not be afraid of the outcomes. This ties in beautifully with the preceding chapter on goal setting. Notice the intricate relationship between the two. The word *courage* in French is *coeur*, and in Spanish, it is *corazon*, and both, when translated, mean "heart." Courage is having the heart to explore your full human potential. We define heart as the willingness to take risks to improve, even in the face of potential failure; the courage to go all out and discover your capability at the moment; and the freedom to lose, learn from it, and forge ahead.

When we think of courage and heart, we remember the brilliant words spoken by Theodore Roosevelt in his 1910 speech "The Man in the Arena":

> It is not the critic who counts; not the man who points out how the strong man stumbles, or where the doer of deeds could have done them better. The credit belongs to the man who is actually in the arena, whose face is marred by dust and sweat and blood; who strives valiantly; who errs, who comes short again and again, because there is not effort without error and shortcoming; but

who does actually strive to do the deeds; who knows great enthu-
siasms, the great devotions; who spends himself in a worthy cause;
who at best knows in the end the triumph of high achievement,
and who at the worst, if he fails, at least fails while daring greatly,
so that his place shall never be with those cold and timid souls
who neither know victory nor defeat.[10]

Champion sports parents and athletes are not timid souls. They are not
afraid of failure because they know that loss and setbacks are great teachers.
They may fail, but they do so by "daring greatly," and they get back up and
try again, wiser and stronger. They show up, which is half the battle. Many
in this world never show up. In championship cultures, everyone is all in
with living the core values and being authentic and vulnerable. Now, that's
what I call awesome courage. And you, as a sports parent, can begin to have
these courageous conversations with your children at any age.

You may want to read Brené Brown's book *Daring Greatly*, a title
taken from Roosevelt's speech. In the book she talks about this great
courage: "We must walk into the arena, whatever it may be . . . with
courage. We must dare to show up and let ourselves be seen."[11] So
many athletes, especially the young ones, hold back, fearful of going all
out because they may look silly, fail, let their team, coach, and parents
down, make a mistake, or not be good enough. A true champion, we've
learned, is willing to dare greatly and jump off the cliff, knowing that
others will "have my back." That's the attitude as a champion sports
parent that you want to convey to your children.

For champion sports parenting, this is the spirit of play. Your athletes
playing only with their heads tend to be too ego-involved, smitten with

---

10 Theodore Roosevelt, "The Man in the Arena," April 23, 1910, at the Sorbonne
in Paris, https://www.theodorerooseveltcenter.org/Learn-About-TR/TR-
Encyclopedia/Culture-and-Society/Man-in-the-Arena.aspx.

11 Brené Brown, *Daring Greatly: How the Courage to Be Vulnerable Transforms the
Way We Live, Love, Parent, and Lead* (New York: Avery, 2015).

themselves and overly concerned with outcomes and winning. Courageous parents and athletes, on the other hand, have a deep desire to win—but if they don't win, they refuse to measure their self-worth by any outcome. According to Olympian gymnast Simone Biles, "Being a gymnast means having the strength to hold on and the courage to let go." Letting go and moving on from defeat is a courageous act. This is a thought you can easily share with your child.

So, how do you instill the value of courageousness in your child? You must give them the freedom to fail. Of course, having the coach on board with this (see Part 3) is most desirable. It's helpful for your children to learn that mistakes and setbacks are necessary components of the improvement process. Learning from failures helps to develop the most challenging, difficult athletic skills. If these kids do not have a positive relationship with failure, they will not take risks and, as a result, come to a full stop on the road to greatness.

When your young athletes fail, suggest that they step back, embrace the failure, and learn from it. Athletes should know that you see failure in this way and courage is the strategic response. When failure of any kind occurs, take the time to ask your athlete, "What did you learn from that situation? What could you do to prevent such mistakes in the future?" Rather than fighting their failures, these child athletes gain from seeing their setbacks as natural occurrences that are necessary if they are to grow and improve. It's nature's way of helping us all to be better versions of ourselves. When they feel devastated from taking a risk and suffering a setback, they can be reassured by you, the parent, that they are about to learn from the experience in some way that will help them improve. If they overlook this lesson or resist learning it, they will create new limitations that will impede their performance.

Specifically, ask your young athletes to demonstrate courage by accepting embarrassment when it comes. This may mean diving for control of a loose ball or coming back after taking a hard fall. It may mean holding their heads high when losing a game if they went all out.

It may involve taking the open shot after having already missed five in a row, facing the crowd on the opponent's home court, and doing the right thing in all situations.

Next, you can set the stage for success by encouraging your athletes to take risks. Risk taking can be fulfilling, exhilarating, and rewarding. Tell them about times when you took risks and how things worked out.

You can also say this to your children: "If you take the risk and experience a setback, think of the impact this setback will have on your life in five years." This helps put it into perspective. In most cases, they will understand that the setback is meaningless aside from the wonderful lessons it can teach.

Remind your children that success is already theirs for having the courage to take the risk. After all, the most damaging or painful risk could very well be *not* taking the risk to improve your life. Tell your children not to ask, "Will this risk create failure?" Instead, tell them it's better to ask, "Will this risk put me in position for major breakthroughs and growth?" The only real failure is remorse created by avoiding taking risks.

> *Man cannot discover new oceans unless he has the*
> *courage to lose sight of the shore.*
> —Andre Gide, philosopher

Questions on the Quest

1. When did you have courage to take a risk and how did it turn out?
2. What risks would you like your kids to take and how will you help them?
3. In what small ways could you model courage for your family?
4. What can you start doing (that you're not doing) to help your child be more courageous?
5. What can you stop doing (that you are doing) to help your child be more courageous?

PART III:

COACHES ARE YOUR ALLIES, NOT YOUR ADVERSARIES

We have to stop using the small percentage of bad coaches as an excuse not to engage with all the good ones.

—Skye Eddy

John chuckles as he remembers one of his first coaching experiences when he moved to Oregon after a coaching stint in Michigan. He had just coached a game for a young boys' team, and the team was doing a post-game cooldown jog and stretch when an angry mom marched across the field. She demanded that he stop punishing the team for losing the game by making them run afterward, completely mistaking the cooldown in preparation for a game the next day as some sort of punishment. John was incredulous as he tried to explain what he was doing, but the most upset person, as you might imagine, was the poor 11-year-old boy whose mom was embarrassing him in front of everyone.

What John came to realize years later was that this interaction had very little to do with him and a lot to do with a youth sports world that had conditioned parents to assume the worst. In their first team meeting after that game, John was questioned about everything from playing time and commitment expectations (appropriate) to tactics, positions, and formations (not appropriate). The parent group had been conditioned to not trust their coaches and to be governed by fear of missing out. Luckily, John was prepared for this and was able to smooth things over and have a great two-year run with those boys. However, the conflict speaks to a bigger issue.

So often parents and coaches take a starting position of treating one another like adversaries instead of allies. In reality, we all likely have the same goals in mind: give the athletes a great experience, help them develop in and out of competition, help them reach their personal and team goals, and have fun doing it. Yet we come out of the gate ready to jump all over one another.

If we do our homework and find the right organization, and we know and understand our role as parents, we can take a different, more helpful approach. We can look at athlete development as a three-legged stool, with athletes, coaches, and parents all needed to provide the right experience. Remove a leg—the stool collapses. And too often the coach/parent legs are not working together to support the child. We can do better.

In this section you will find ideas on finding the right environment for your child, setting proper coach/parent boundaries, and communicating effectively and appropriately with your coach. We will discuss the vital element of trust, how to give insight to your coach about what is happening to your child on and off the field, and determining when you should intervene (because it is dangerous), or just need to sit back (because it is difficult and challenging). And finally, our children hear what we say, but they remember what we do, so we must model the right behavior when it comes to our interactions with coaches, opponents, and opposing parents.

CHAPTER 22:

FIND THE RIGHT FIT

It's not hard to make decisions when you know what your values are.
—Dr. Ben Freakley, mental performance coach

Do a Google search for youth sports organizations in your area, and it won't be hard to find a winning-comes-first organization in the youth sports world saying something like this:

> Over the past five years, we have won 19 state championships. Our teams go to tournaments with hundreds of college scouts lining the sidelines. Most of our players go on to play in college and get a scholarship to do so, and we have these kids come back and talk to your kids about what it is like. We provide the environment for the elite players who are serious about taking their game to the next level.

We're not saying that this organization is unethical, or is not developing players, or that winning is a bad thing. All we're trying to point out is this: Can you picture your future child playing in front of college scouts? Can you picture her playing in college or raising a state championship trophy? When you pull back the curtain and look at how the sausage is made, often it exposes an ugly underbelly. Most kids who start out with the club at 9 years old are no longer around at 18. Many kids have been injured, have burned out, or have quit. Many children have encountered abusive coaching in pursuit of these scholarships and trophies. Many children end up with lifelong physical and psychological issues due to their youth sports experiences.

We can and must do better, and that starts with enrolling your child in organizations that align with your values for not only athletic development, but human development. The reality is many of us spend much more time researching and reading reviews about our electrician or plumber than we do about our child's sports coach, who is likely to have a huge impact on their life.

Instead, seek out a transformational coach and organization.

Transformational coaches and organizations put the needs of the child athlete above the needs of the business. They focus on developing the total person. They demand that coaches are trained and held to a standard of excellence. Transformational coaches are trusted not only for their sport-specific ability, but for their dependability and connection with athletes. They are evaluated and trained in motivation, communication, and being a positive role model. Individual athletes and teams come first, and the needs of the coach and club come second. The club does these things because its leadership and membership demand it.

Why don't more of our youth sports organizations do the same? Why don't we demand it of them? Why do we settle for shelling out thousands of dollars for a transactional relationship when sport could be so much more? Here are a few things we should demand from our coaches and youth sports organizations:

- Stop only coaching the sport, and coach the person.
- Focus on well-defined core values and intentionally teach them through sports by living them every day and holding athletes, coaches, and parents accountable for knowing and implementing these values.
- Be as intentional at teaching character as at teaching skills.
- Stop using the small number of bad parents as an excuse to not engage the large numbers of good ones.
- Allow kids to follow their own path, especially when it comes to participating in multiple sports at young ages.
- Be patient when it comes to development, and don't be in such a hurry to make cuts, form all-star teams, and travel long distances to play.
- Put the needs of the child in sport ahead of the needs of the business of sport.
- Find ways to connect/collaborate with players and parents beyond the games and practices.

If you take the time and energy to do your homework, much like you might do with a contractor or landscaper, you are far more likely to find an organization and coaches aligned with the values you want to promote and the reasons you signed your child up for sports in the first place. A little legwork up front can save you a lot of heartache in the long run.

Just as your car runs more smoothly and requires less energy to go faster and farther when the wheels are in perfect alignment, you perform better when your thoughts, feelings, emotions, goals, and values are in balance.
—Brian Tracy

Questions on the Quest

1. What is the most important lesson you learned from this chapter?
2. How can this lesson be applied to your child's sports experiences?
3. What can you start doing (that you're not doing) to find the best fit for your child?
4. What can you stop doing (that you are currently doing) to find the best fit for your child?
5. What are the ideals and values you want sports to develop and prompt in your child? Come up with a "Sports Mission Statement" for your family. Then go find an organization that is aligned with these values.

CHAPTER 23:

KNOW YOUR ROLE

When you attend a sporting event, you can have only one role.
You can be an athlete, a coach, an official, or a spectator.
Never more than one.

—Bruce Brown

Imagine the perfect summer day.[12] The sun is out. The birds are chirping. And a bunch of 7-year-old boys scurry about a baseball diamond, trying to hit, run, throw and catch, all the while smiling and giggling and doing what 7-year-old boys do.

But then the game gets tense. Parents and coaches started chirping at each other, at the players, and at the umpire. A call is missed. Then another. The situation worsens.

The umpire, a 13-year-old named Josh Cordova—who umpires so he can pay for his own baseball equipment, by the way—warns both coaches and their fans. Yet the tension escalates. Parents are dropping

---

12 "When You Attend a Youth Sports Event, Know Your Role!", Changing the Game Project, https://changingthegameproject.com/when-you-attend-a-youth-sports-event-know-your-role/.

F-bombs and pointing fingers trying to get others thrown out. Finally, all hell breaks loose. Coaches argue. Parents get into it with one another. And it ends in a fight that goes viral across the globe. Five people were arrested. Two were suspended from their jobs. And Cordova, when interviewed after the game, said the following: "I was scared not only for me but the 7-year-olds who happened to be on the field at the time. We never thought anyone would fight at a little league baseball game. I thought maybe by issuing a warning everyone would just chill, take a step back and realize how stupid they were acting … but [I] guess not."

A perfect summer day ended in assault charges and public shaming. Why? What is wrong with us when people go to jail over things that happen at a 7-year-olds' baseball game? Since when did the results of a 7-year-olds' baseball game matter? And if we have developmental baseball players, then we also are going to have developmental officials and coaches. Mistakes are supposed to be made.

When you attend a sporting event, you can be one of four things:

- A coach, who leads and organizes the athletes
- An athlete, who participates in the competition
- A fan, who cheers on the participants
- An official/referee, who applies the rules to the best of his/her ability

That's it. You cannot be more than one at the same time. Each role has certain responsibilities, and if you try to be a fan plus one of these other roles, things get messy and stress levels increase. For example, I see this a lot at youth sporting events:

The Fan Coach: We all know the parent who keeps a running dialogue with their child and gives instructions on every play. If you are not the team coach, and you have dropped your daughter off at training all week and gone about your business, then do not coach her come game time. It does not help her if you arrive on Saturday and start telling her and her teammates where to run, how to hit, where to pass, or when to shoot. The reason we only have one teacher in school is so kids do not get confused by conflicting instructions in the classroom. Imagine if there were 28 sets of parents there every day during math. Come game day, though, often the head coach is drowned out by the 16 parent-coaches yelling conflicting instructions to the players on the field. The result, more often than not, is not action but inaction from the players.

The Fan Official: We all know this person as well. He may be 75 yards away from the play, while the actual umpire or referee is a few feet away, but clearly he saw it better. When you're watching your child's sporting event, you must remember that you are there as a fan and not to officiate. When you live and die with every call, when you scream in disagreement at an official decision, you not only make the environment a negative learning one for your child, but you set an incredibly poor example for him. So the next time a ball goes out for a throw-in or a corner kick and you think it is the wrong call, ask yourself, "Does it really even matter? Will anyone actually remember this game 6 months from now?"

The Coach Referee: Instead of coaching his or her players, the coach-referee lives and dies with every call, argues for pointless strikes or outs, and often makes a fool of himself, embarrasses his players, and gets everyone riled up about nothing. It's youth sport. It's about the kids. If you want to referee, then please, by all means referee. You are needed! But if you are going to coach, then coach and leave the refereeing to someone else.

We need to know our role. We can play, we can coach, we can officiate, or we can be a fan. In my experience, every incident that happens at a youth sporting event usually happens when a person, typically an adult, tries to take on multiple roles. It may be innocuous sideline coaching that infuriates a coach or another parent. It may be a seemingly innocent comment directed at an opposing player. It can be vocal disrespect for a referee. It usually starts small, but often these things escalate, and next thing you know, you have police at a 7-year-olds' baseball game, leading dads away in cuffs. A day that started like any other beautiful summer day ends in tragedy for those poor kids playing and a young umpire trying to earn a few extra bucks. This day will be remembered forever by all who attended. Sadly, it will be remembered for all the wrong reasons.

Remember, change starts at home. Next time you attend a youth sports event, know your role and stick to it. Let the kids play! Let the coaches coach. And let the officials officiate. The children will appreciate you for it.

Knowing yourself is the beginning of all wisdom.
—Aristotle

Questions on the Quest

1. What is the most important lesson you learned from this chapter?
2. How can this lesson be applied in all your future sports spectating experiences?
3. What can you start doing (that you're not doing) to accept your role at your child's sporting events?
4. What can you stop doing (that you are currently doing) to accept your role at your child's sporting events?

CHAPTER 24:

SET PROPER BOUNDARIES

The only people who get upset about you setting boundaries
are the ones who were benefiting from you having none.

—Unknown

The opening story of Part III is a perfect illustration of role confusion and lack of proper boundaries in the coach-parent relationship. Every parent-coach relationship should have proper boundaries in place. No coach should be expected to discuss every issue, at all hours of the day and night, nor should a coach have the right to ignore and give no feedback at all to a parent. Obviously, the older your child gets, the less important your role as a parent becomes as your child learns to have adult conversations and navigate their own journey. And this starts with setting boundaries and expectations that are age- and ability-appropriate for the parent-coach relationship.

It is imperative for coaches to set appropriate boundaries that define how and when they will interact with parents, the topics they will discuss, and the ones they will not. This is very important and not something to be dealt with in highly emotional situations such as post-game, post-tryouts, etc. Having guidelines that are clear, consistently enforced, written down, and provided for parents is a huge first step in defining and developing the coach-parent relationship. Every team, coach, and club will likely have their own specific boundaries, but here are some we have found useful:

The 24-hour rule: Many people are emotional after an athletic event, so we suggest that parents and coaches wait 24 hours before having a conversation, firing off an email, or, worst of all, posting something on social media they will later regret. Giving everyone a day or two before dealing with a difficult situation—such as playing time, role on the team, something you may or may not have said, etc.—is the best way to ensure your meeting or conversation will be constructive.

Office hours and other appropriate times to connect: No one should be available 24/7. Everyone, especially coaches, deserves downtime and family time. There should be agreed-upon times to communicate and respond to inquiries.

Outline of philosophy, commitment, and playing time expectations: Coaches should articulate this up front so there is no confusion. When John's daughter used to play club volleyball, he read on their website that on their travel teams—which flew across the United States beginning at 12 years old—not a single minute of playing time was guaranteed. Yup, fly five hours each way, spend thousands of dollars, and don't get any playing time. While he unequivocally disagrees with this shortsighted and sport-destroying policy, at least they put it front and center on their website. If you still signed your kid up, well, then you got what you paid for.

Things that coaches will discuss with a parent:

- Playing time
- Your child's performance
- Things to work on at home
- A personal improvement plan for the child
- Issues that may be affecting a child's performance, which may include behavior from other team members but nothing sport-specific (i.e., bullying)

Things that coaches will not discuss with a parent:

- Anything related to the performance of another child on the team
- Tactics
- Practice planning and session topics
- Substitutions, playing styles

Setting and agreeing to appropriate boundaries between coaches and parents is not a burden. It actually will provide a greater sense of respect, understanding, and collaboration and allow you to work together to benefit your athletes. When coaches and parents stop "dealing" with one another and instead "engage" with one another, great things happen.

Find out if your coach/club/school has written guidelines and boundaries for the coach-parent relationship. If not, perhaps you can help to craft them in collaboration with the coaching staff.

> *The more you value yourself, the healthier your boundaries are.*
> —Lorraine Nilon, self-help author and podcaster

Questions on the Quest

1. What is your biggest takeaway from this chapter, and how can you apply that lesson?
2. What do you need to start doing (that you aren't doing) to set proper boundaries with your child's coach?
3. What do you need to stop doing (that you are doing) to establish better boundaries in your coach–parent relationship?

CHAPTER 25:

EFFECTIVELY COMMUNICATE

The single biggest problem in communication is the illusion it has taken place.
—George Bernard Shaw

John has been coaching long enough to have been on the receiving end of many angry emails, texts, phone calls, and meetings, as well as countless positive ones. And what he has learned is that, as George Bernard Shaw describes above, the greatest problem with communication is the illusion it has taken place. Yet great communication is the key to the parent–coach relationship.

John has written extensively about parent-child communication in his book *Changing the Game*, and many of the same principles apply to your relationship with your child's coach. If you are going to have positive communication with your child's coach, try following some of these principles:

Be an Active Listener: Communication expert Betsy Butterick joined John and Jerry on the *Way of Champions Podcast*, Episode 202, in 2021 and suggested that whenever they approach a conversation, they ask themselves, "What can I learn here?" This question is a powerful tool to get you actively engaged in what the other person is saying. What emotions is your coach expressing? What are they asking of you? Are they relaxed or defensive? And when you do speak, ask open-ended questions that require a longer answer.

Paraphrase Their Main Points: When responding to something the coach says, try to paraphrase their main points so you can confirm that what you are hearing is what they are trying to convey. It tells the coach you are listening, and it allows them to correct you if you have misunderstood what they are trying to tell you. You will never have a path forward unless you know what everyone is asking.

Respect Their Emotions and Control Your Own: One of the reasons we advocate for a 24-hour rule before engaging in any conversation is to allow emotions to cool. Whether you need to exercise, meditate, pray, or whatever it takes, trying to control your emotions before a difficult conversation with a coach is huge. Give yourself enough time to be calm before any conversation so you move beyond reacting and become better at responding. At the same time, respect the coach's emotions as well by giving them the time and space to set up a meeting or call. Use what is called emotional labeling, such as "I see you are angry" or "I see this upsets you" to gain clarity and make the coach feel heard. Emotional meetings are often the least productive.

Use "I" Statements: It is very easy to use accusatory "you" statements that tend to put people on the defensive. "You are ruining my child's experience" or "You are playing favorites" will shut down communication—or worse, cause your coach to attack you back, and the conversation will soon fall apart. Instead, use "I" statements such as "I feel frustrated when my son doesn't get any meaningful playing time" or "I am struggling to understand what my daughter can do to earn a starting spot." "I" statements allow you to express how you are feeling without blaming the coach and putting them on the defensive.

Be Consistent: Whether it's your behavior, your communication, or your interactions with the coach, do your best to be consistent. Nothing is worse for a coach to have a parent who is collegial one day and calling for their head the next. By developing your relationship and trust in each other, and not making faulty assumptions about each other's intentions, you will have far more productive conversations.

Avoid Electronic Communications Whenever Possible: In our experience, the best way to handle difficult conversations is face-to-face. We realize it is becoming a lost art in this day and age, but it is so crucial. We cannot tell you how many times we have seen something minor blow up into a major incident because a hastily composed email or text message does not convey emotion or tone and is misconstrued. Try to meet in person, or at least have a phone call. John has a rule that the longer and angrier the email or text, the shorter his response, often distilled down to a few words: "Do you have time for a call?" And finally, never air your grievances on social media. You may get some sympathetic pats on the back from friends, but you will alienate your coach.

In 99 percent of cases, coaches and parents have the same positive intentions for their athletes and teams. Being able to effectively communicate with one another, not only when things are going well but also when there is uncertainty, struggle, and growth, is a key to a positive sports experience. Make sure your communication has actually taken place.

> *Most of the successful people I've known are the ones*
> *who do more listening than talking.*
> —Bernard Baruch

Questions on the Quest

1. What is your biggest lesson learned from this chapter, and how can you apply it in the future?
2. How can you better prepare ahead of time for difficult conversations?
3. What do you need to start doing (that you're not doing) to promote better communication with your child's coach?
4. What do you need to stop doing (that you are doing) to improve communication with your child's coach?

CHAPTER 26:

BUILD TRUST

Trust is like the air we breathe. When it's present no one notices,
and when it's absent everyone can see it.

—Warren Buffett

Jean-Francois Gravelet was born in 1824 in St. Omey, Pas-de-Calais, France. From a young age, he showed great aptitude in balance, strength, and agility, and at age 5 he was sent to the acrobatics school in Lyon. After only a few months of training, he gave his first performance and was soon dubbed the "Boy Wonder." As he grew, so did his fame, and soon the world came to know him by a different name: the Great Blondin.

Gravelet (or Charles Blondin, as he often went by) traveled from France to North America in 1855, where he became part owner of a traveling circus. Then, on June 30, 1859, his fame and fortune took a turn for the better. On that day, Blondin crossed the 1,100-foot Niagara Gorge stretching from the United States to Canada, balancing on a 3.5-inch tightrope and suspended 160 feet above the raging falls. The Great Blondin became a legend.

Blondin became world-famous with his Niagara Falls escapades, and every year he would return to the falls and up the ante. He crossed blindfolded. He stood on a chair with only one leg balanced on the rope. He walked on stilts. He carried his manager, Harry Colcord, across the falls on his back. One year, he even stopped halfway, sat down, and cooked and ate an omelet.

But for our purposes in this book, one crossing stands out. Blondin, ever the showman, showed up with a wheelbarrow with a staff welded to it. You can picture the scene as the great showman revved up the crowd of 10,000-plus, saying, "Who thinks the Great Blondin can walk across the falls on this rope?" Can you imagine the scene as the crowd cheered loudly, perhaps even chanting his name, "Blondin, Blondin, Blondin!"?

Then Blondin asked the crowd, "Who thinks I can push this cart across the falls?" They cheered louder still.

Then came the kicker: "Who wants to get in the cart?"

Crickets. Not a peep. Some nervous laughter and looks of "Is he serious?" No one volunteered to get in the cart.

The entire crowd believed that Blondin had the ability to push the cart across the falls. But they still didn't trust him—because trust goes way beyond ability. They had no connection to him. They had no idea about him as a person. They didn't know whether he was believable or reliable.[13]

That's the essence of trust. It's not simply about ability. It's about connection, believability, and vulnerability. If athletic development is a three-legged stool in which the athlete, the coach, and the parent are all working hard to uphold the stool, then trust is the glue that holds it all together. Without trust in those three relationships, the stool will collapse.

Today's sports culture often erodes trust. The demands for early specialization, the high costs and high commitments at young ages,

---

13 Excerpted from *Every Moment Matters p 269-270*

the outcome-focused goals on titles and scholarships in preadolescent sports—all of these erode trust and turn what could be a transformational sporting experience into a transactional one. It's easy to imagine ulterior motives from our coaches or clubs, even though in most instances there are none.

We must think of trust like a bank account. We want to put as many deposits as possible into that account with both our athletes and coaches, so that when we need to make withdrawals, we have a balance. If a new parent comes storming out of the gate, demanding many things before any relationship has been built, a coach is likely to pull back, dismiss the parent as "one of those parents"—and trust is broken before it ever had a chance.

So what is trust?

In his book *The Speed of Trust*, author Stephen M.R. Covey explains that trust either adds a dividend or extracts a tax from every activity we do and every dimension of a relationship. If you are going to build a high-trust relationship with a coach, you must be worthy of trust. To do so, Covey has a list of specific behaviors, including:

- Talk straight and tell the truth.
- Demonstrate concern and genuinely care for others.
- Be transparent.
- Make things right when you are wrong.
- Show loyalty and give credit to others.
- Don't skirt the real issues, even the tough ones.
- Be clear with your expectations.
- Be accountable.
- Listen before you speak.
- Fulfill your commitments.
- Extend trust in abundance to others. [14]

---

14   https://saom.memberclicks.net/assets/SAM_unpublished_links/13-Behaviors-Hand- out-CoveyLink.pdf.

It is pretty clear that if you follow Covey's guidelines, you are far more likely to build a high-trust relationship with any coach. And if not, it is likely no fault of your own.

When your child has a new coach, reach out, say hello, volunteer to help if you're able, and then let them settle in. Once the season gets going, be mindful of the following things:

- Respect the coach's time: He or she may have a family, another job, and certainly a life away from your child, so be respectful of boundaries. Do not call or email at all hours of the night. Remember that the coach has 10 to 50 athletes on the team, while your concern is for one of them. Ask yourself, "If every parent sent the same number of texts/emails as I did, would the coach have any free time?" Of course you should communicate, but pick and choose your moments.
- Respect boundaries: Respect the team rules and boundaries regarding communication, locations, and timing for conversations and topics of conversation.
- Don't assume the worst: So often trust is broken over simple misunderstandings. Before you get too excited, reach out in a calm fashion to find out exactly what happened in a certain situation. Parents who are overly emotional and short-fused rarely build the kind of trust with coaches needed for a successful relationship.

Trust is the glue of life. It's the most essential ingredient in effective communication. It's the foundational principle that holds all relationships.
—Stephen R. Covey

Questions on the Quest

1. What is your most important lesson learned from this chapter, and how can this lesson be applied?
2. What can you start doing (that you're not doing) to build trust with your child's coaches?
3. What can you stop doing (that you are currently doing) to build trust with your child's coaches?

CHAPTER 27:

GIVE THE COACH INSIGHT INTO YOUR CHILD

You never really understand a person until you consider things from his point of view.

—Harper Lee

John can recall very vividly one of his worst coaching moments. It occurred many years ago while he was coaching a team of U17 girls in Bend, Oregon. One of his top players was having a very poor training session. It was not like her to be a bit lazy and unfocused, and since the entire group was struggling that day and a big tournament was coming up, John was growing irate. He finally snapped at the player, and the tears rolled down her cheeks as she apologized for her performance. Yet nothing changed.

John felt a tap on his shoulder as one of his team captains pulled him aside. "Her grandma passed away this morning. You know how close they were. You need to cut her some slack."

John felt horrible. Of course he needed to cut her some slack. He knew her grandma and how close they were. In fact, the prior summer, the entire team shared a meal and a dip in the pool at Grandma's house in California while at an event. John was devastated as well. Yet how was he to know what was going on with her off the field so he could be a better coach for her on the field?

Throughout their careers, John and Jerry have encountered numerous parents with very difficult off-field issues such as illness, divorce, financial struggles, and more. And they've been amazed at how often they ask, "Did you let the coach know?" and the families say they have not. They are afraid the coach will think they are making excuses, or the kids are soft and should get over it, or the coach will use it against them. Instead they send their kids to training in a poor state of mind with a poorly informed coach. It is a recipe for disaster.

Obviously there are coaches out there who do not care; there are bad people in every profession. But the vast majority of coaches want this information and will be more than understanding when an adverse situation arises. Even if your child still attends training or games, the coach will have a better understanding of why their performance might not be their best.

Parents, your child's coach has a large number of players to pay attention to, while your attention is almost solely focused on one child: yours. You are going to see things and hear things and know things the coach cannot possibly understand or know, so inform them. Give them insight. If your child gets into the car and bursts into tears because of something that happened on the field, let the coach know. If you are getting divorced, or Dad has cancer, or Grandma passed away, let the coach know. You will find empathy and compassion far more often than an uncaring response. And if the response is dispassionate, that certainly tells you how much that coach values the person versus the athlete. Not much at all.

The improvement of the understanding is for two ends;
first, for our own increase of knowledge; secondly,
to enable us to deliver and make out that
knowledge to others.
—John Locke

Questions on the Quest

1. What was the biggest lesson you learned from this chapter, and how can you apply it?
2. What do you need to start doing (that you aren't doing) to give the coach more insight into your child?
3. What do you need to stop doing (that you are doing) that is hindering the coach's ability to understand what is happening to your child on and off the field?

CHAPTER 28:

WHEN TO LET GO AND WHEN TO INTERVENE

Sometimes letting things go is an act of far greater power than hanging on.

—Eckhart Tolle

Jenny Levy knows a thing or two about coaching and building a successful sports program. A former All-American lacrosse player herself and a 2021 inductee into the National Lacrosse Hall of Fame, she is now head coach at the University of North Carolina. She has won. A lot. As in over 400 games, three NCAA titles, 7 ACC titles, 13 NCAA Final Fours, and as of this writing 24 straight NCAA tournament appearances. She also has three kids with her husband, Dan, a former Tar Heel national champion lacrosse player, and all three are NCAA lacrosse players at Carolina. So, needless to say, Jenny and Dan know a thing or two about parenting young athletes as well. That's why her advice a few years back on our podcast was so interesting.[15]

---

15 Coach Jenny Levy, *Changing the Game Project* podcast, Episode 23, https://changingthegameproject.com/woc-23-jenny-levy-two-time-national-lacrosse-champion-coach-year-not-winning-atmosphere-matters/).

As her multi-sport kids grew up, Jenny and Dan had a variety of coaches for their kids, from volunteer to paid professions. It's important when we put our kids in sports, says Levy, to support your kids, love them, and be an advocate for them when necessary. But regardless of the coach, whether you agree with them or not when it comes to strategy on the field and the Xs and Os, it's important to teach your kids to be respectful and do what the coach asks. "There is some stuff that coaches have done that [causes] my husband and I [to] scratch our heads, but they are the coach; it's their vision. We are going to teach our young people that even if they disagree, find a way to have a win–win," she says.

There are plenty of times when the disagreement you may have with a coach is an "Xs and Os" issue. It may be the position they are playing, playing time, how practices are structured, or game formations. Even if you know a lot about the sport, if you do not have the time to be out there coaching, you really need to take a step back and let your child learn something else. "We have seen all sorts of things," says Levy, "and some of it's a growing process for our children. If [we] are constantly stepping in and being right, we are sending the message to the kids that it's my way or the highway, and it doesn't give our kids a lot of resilience."

On the other hand, when it comes to the cultural side of things—the treatment of human beings—that would be a moment where Levy and her husband, as well as all parents, should consider stepping in. "If it's gotten to a point where it's detrimental to our child on the values side of things, that's where we might step in," she says. This is great advice.

There are coaches who cross the line from demanding to demeaning. There are coaches and environments in which an athlete's humanity is critiqued instead of a technical or tactical error. There are cases of bullying, of emotional and physical abuse. Clearly, these are times when a parent must step in. When the physical, emotional, and mental safety of a child is at stake, you intervene.

This seems easy, but is it? As we have seen with numerous scandals across sports such as figure skating, gymnastics, swimming, and soccer, many parents are afraid to intervene at times because they are afraid to threaten their child's position on a team, a chance for the Olympics, or the opportunity to be recruited for an NCAA team. And if it's not easy in these situations, how about all the gray areas and knowing the difference between a difficult situation and a dangerous one?

For better or for worse, this is parenting in a nutshell. We are constantly walking the line between difficult and dangerous with our kids, both inside and outside of sports. We are constantly asking ourselves, "Is this a moment to let this blow up in their face so they learn, develop some resilience, and move on, or is this too dangerous to not intervene?" There is no perfect answer, no exact science. It's hard, and only in hindsight will we know if we were right or wrong.

What we can do is walk alongside our kids on this journey, discuss each situation, explain where the learning opportunities may come from, and keep communicating. Sometimes it may go from difficult to dangerous, and you must be ready to act. But for the most part, take a deep breath, and choose to let go rather than hang on, especially when it has to do with the Xs and Os. You'll be glad you did.

> *Feel everything. Let go of everything.*
> *Or you will be held captive by everything.*
> —Unknown

Questions on the Quest

1. What was the biggest lesson you learned in this chapter, and how can you apply it?
2. Ask your child what they would like you to say and do on the sidelines or in the stands. Do they like it when you cheer? Do they like

it when you shout instructions (doubtful)? Ask them how you can best support their journey.

3. What do you need to start doing (that you aren't doing) to let go and let the sports experience belong to your child?

4. What do you need to stop doing (that you are doing) to let go and let the sports experience belong to your child??

PART IV:

GAME DAY CHAMPION PARENT BEHAVIORS

I've learned that people will forget what you said, people will forget what you did, but people will never forget how you made them feel.

— Maya Angelou

Jill Ellis is the all-time winningest coach in US Women's National Soccer team history. She won two World Cups (2015 and 2019) and was twice named FIFA International Coach of the Year. She coached some of the greatest athletes the game has seen. She oversaw both great successes and failures (such as the 2016 Rio Olympics). When you watch her coach, you observe her incredible technical and tactical knowledge, but the one thing that stands out to us is her incredibly calm sideline demeanor.

Jill Ellis, in the most chaotic moments, stands there serene. She's not barking orders up and down the sideline; she isn't waving her hands or drawing attention to herself. She is calm, cool, and collected, just like she wants her players to be. It's a trait she says she got from her mom.

"I think what I saw in my mom was a consistency in her behavior," Ellis told Michal Gervais on his *Finding Mastery* podcast.

> I don't remember her ever losing it or being emotional. I remember being on the sideline and seeing one of my assistant coaches being incredibly emotional. And I thought to myself, *If I ever coach, I want to be so steady on that sideline that the team never thinks I'm not with them at that moment.* So I tried to . . . and as a young coach, I didn't master that for sure, but I think trying to be as consistent as I could with my players was something that was important.[16]

Ellis wasn't always perfect at this. She recalls how, in her younger days and as coach of UCLA for 12 years, she would lose it from time to time, most often at referees. But as she grew into her coaching, she realized that was not helpful to her players or to her program. "Those emotions come out, and yeah, I have a hard time kind of keeping those in," she told Gervais. "And then I realized that's just expended energy. What I learned, the higher I went up in the coaching . . . was you can't miss a second. You can't waste your emotion because you have to make a decision. It's the next decision is what you need to be focused on."

Part IV is all about modeling the right behaviors pre-, post-, and during competition for our kids. We all intuitively understand that being calm, cool, and collected would be great for our kids. We all want to do our part to get them ready pregame, and say and do the right things postgame, especially after a tough loss. Yet sometimes this is hard, as we will learn in the next few chapters. Champion sports parents are great at creating the right environment for their kids pre-competition, during the heat of battle, and when the event is completed.

The next few chapters outline some specific pre-competition,

---

16 Jill Ellis, Episode 245: "The Pressure of Coaching the U.S. Women's National Soccer Team," https://findingmastery.com/podcasts/jill-ellis/.

during-competition, and post-competition behaviors that science, research, athlete interviews, and pure common sense tell us will give your child the best chance of having a positive competition experience. We will list specific, action-oriented behaviors on how to apply what you have learned. Modeling the right behaviors and acting the way you want your child and their team to act—and hopefully getting the other coaches and spectators to do the same—is a crucial component of being a champion sports parent. Because, as Maya Angelou says, what they will remember most was how the experience made them feel. Good luck!

CHAPTER 29:

DON'T PULL A HAMMY: SUGGESTED PRE-COMPETITION BEHAVIORS

Most battles are won before they are fought.

—Sun Tzu

Many years ago, John was coaching a soccer team made up of middle school-aged girls. The team would practice well and play great at home, but on away game days, the same group of top performers would often struggle. He couldn't figure it out until one day he realized that these girls always carpooled together to away games, and one dad was usually the driver. What was happening in that car?

Upon asking one of the girls, John learned that the dad would spend the ride talking about the opponent, their record, the teams they beat, and so on. You can imagine the conversation: "This team is 12-0, they have outscored their opponents 34-1, and their forward is on the national team. But go get 'em, ladies, you got this!" By the time the girls got to the field, they were already toast, with thoughts of playing against giant, unbeatable opponents dancing through their heads.

This dad was well intentioned and genuinely excited for the girls, but his actions prior to the game were not helping at all. In fact, they were hurting the team's performance. Once John learned this, he pulled the dad aside, explained that what he was doing was actually having a negative effect on the kids, and gave him some of the tips we discuss in this chapter. Lo and behold, a quiet dad and child-centric car ride started to change behavior. Below are a couple of pregame behaviors we have found that will help your child perform their very best.

Develop a Pre-Event Routine: Have you ever watched a professional golfer before a shot or a basketball player before a free throw? Have you noticed that they have a pre-shot routine? The purpose of this is to calm and steady themselves and give them confidence that they have done this before. Together with your child, develop a pre-game checklist that may include things such as proper sleep the night before, packing their uniform and bag, hydration, nutrition, and some mindfulness or visualization. This routine gives your kids accountability (so they don't forget stuff) as well as ownership. Are they waiting for the game . . . or preparing for the game? A pre-competition routine delivers consistency in the experience, with the same routine prior to every event, regardless of its implications.

Remember That Feelings Equal Function: As we wrote about in Parts I and II, how athletes feel often determines how they function. If they are tight, tense, and tentative pre-competition, it does not usually set the stage for high performance. So many kids have a performance-based identity, thinking their worth is tied up in winning or losing, accolades, and championships. Of course, our love for our kids is not determined by those outcomes, but society often tells them otherwise. So what do we do? Bathe them in the RIVER (see chapter 7).

Through your words and actions, help them feel relevant, important, valued, empowered, and respected. As a reminder, some RIVER statements include:

- You're important to us and your team. They need your awesome efforts.
- I love your work ethic. It motivates all of us.
- You bring out the best in everyone.
- That last week of practice was one of your best thus far. When you practice like that, you're being a true champion.
- I appreciate and love how much you give of yourself to your teammates.
- Whether you win or lose, I love you no matter what.

Refrain from Giving Unsolicited Advice: Much like the dad in John's story, well-intentioned parents often think they are helping by giving technical, tactical, and preparation advice to their kids. And sometimes they are, but many times their advice is not wanted and has the opposite effect. As they say, when the student is ready, the teacher will appear, yet so often as parents we want to make something a teachable moment that is not. All those statistics about the opponent? Probably not helpful, and if they were, the coach would have covered them in training. All your words to get your kids excited and hyped for the game (because you are)? Potentially causing stress and anxiety because they see how much this game means to you, and they don't want to let you down.

Now, if your child asks for advice, input, and ideas, by all means give them. But be clear, concise, and brief. Ask them questions to solicit their own answers and understanding. Tune in to their questions and demeanor, and don't overdo it. Potentially make it part of your pre-competition routine, but only after asking, "Do you want some input?" Let them drive the bus on this one, and when they are ready to stop talking about it, let it go. Research shows that athletes rarely remember more than one or two things in pregame and halftime talks, so it's likely they won't remember most of what you say anyway. Pick the one or two most important points and get those across.

Get Them Off Their Screens: As our world has become more narrowly focused on the small devices we hold in our pockets and call smartphones and device use has become ubiquitous for adults and children alike, many a child spends hours before a sports competition staring at the screen in their hands. Is playing video games, or watching a movie on a screen on the ride to the game a good thing? Research says no for two reasons.

First, Malaysian sport scientists found that screen time, which causes mental fatigue, inhibits skilled sport performance.[17] The researchers found that activities such as social media scrolling, videos, and other cognitively exhausting activities negatively affect perception of effort and speed to complete a skillful task. Soccer defenders showed less perceptual awareness and made less successful tackles, while basketball players committed more turnovers when cognitively exhausted.

Neuroscientist Michael Merzneich found that as we spend more time on our screens, we develop tunnel vision and less awareness of our surroundings. Our brains acclimatize to the small-screen view, and we dull our capacity to see beyond that limited space. Clearly, especially in team and invasion sports, where understanding of space, teammates, and opponents is critical, the less perceptual acuity an athlete has, the worse they will perform.

Explain the issues of mental fatigue and tunnel vision to your children, and at least get them to agree to turning off their videos and

---

17 He Sun, Kim Geok Soh, Samsilah Roslan, Mohd Rozilee Wazir Norjali Wazir, Kim Lam Soh, "Does Mental Fatigue Affect Skilled Performance in Athletes? A Systematic Review," October 14, 2021, PlosOne, https://journals.plos.org/plosone/article?id=10.1371/journal.pone.0258307#ack.

social media a minimum of 2 hours prior to competition. They are still welcome to listen to music or a podcast, but ask them to pick their heads up and see the world around them.

Sometimes the game is won before it even begins, and sometimes it is already lost. Often that is due to the pregame environment we create for our kids. So work with your child to develop a pregame routine that includes nutrition, hydration, packing their gear, and some mindfulness/visualization. Bathe them in the RIVER so they know you love them no matter what. Refrain from giving advice unless asked. Remember that how they feel often determines how they function. And finally, get them off their screens. That is a high-performance pregame environment.

> *You've got to win in your mind before you win in your life.*
> —John Addison, keynote speaker and bestselling author

Questions on the Quest

1. What is your biggest takeaway from this chapter, and how can you apply it?
2. What do you need to start doing (that you aren't doing) to help your child prepare for competition?
3. What do you need to stop doing (that you are doing) to help your child better prepare for competition?

CHAPTER 30:

IT'S NOT AN EMERGENCY: ESSENTIAL BEHAVIORS DURING COMPETITION

One of the scariest things for me is to sit on the sidelines of youth soccer or youth lacrosse or poolside, just listening to the things parents say to their kids. And I am sure if I videotaped them, and played it back to them, they would be appalled.
—Dr. Jim Taylor, internationally recognized authority on the psychology of performance, sport, and parenting

Have you ever noticed when you go to your child's game that you react one way to bad calls, aggressive fouls, or intense situations in your game but have little or no reaction to similar situations in the game prior to yours, in which you have no emotional stake? You can sit there with a neutral demeanor while your child warms up, watching two teams hack each other to pieces while the referee turns a blind eye, yet feel nothing. But once your child's game kicks off, your emotions rise, the tension heightens, and everything changes.

If your answer is yes, you are perfectly normal. How normal? Well, a Google search for the term "parents acting badly at sports events" returns 33 million results! Nearly every parent, player, and coach goes through these same emotions. Science tells us why: mirror processing.

In the 1990s, Italian researchers stumbled upon a class of neurons in the brain that fire not only when an individual performs an action, but also when that individual witnesses another person perform an action. This is why we yawn when we see others yawn, or flinch when we see someone stub a toe. Do you ever smile when you see someone smile? These reactions are governed by your mirror neurons, which allow you to not only simulate the actions of others, but also the emotions behind those actions! Researchers have used fMRI technology to test the effect of emotional attachment on brain function, and the results are extraordinary.

When you are watching a loved one participate in an athletic contest, or even watching your favorite college football team play on Saturday, you are actually using a different region of your brain to judge a pass interference or offsides call than you would use in a neutral situation! The neutral decision makes areas of your brain actually disengage, so you use your inferior parietal lobe (IPL). The result: Your brain reacts *as if you were* the one performing the action. That's why we lose our heads so often at our kid's games. Our brains react as we were being fouled or unjustly having a goal called back.

The same mirror processing that governs our behavior is also the reason teams feed off one another's energy, often either peaking and dominating together or sulking and giving up at the same time. Team emotions are contagious, both in a positive and negative way!

So, what does this mean for us? First of all, as adults involved in youth sports, it's good to know there is a scientific explanation for our sudden emotional change. It is up to us to prevent this from becoming a behavioral change as well. We must recognize that if we are intense and out of control, our players likely will mirror that behavior.

By the same token, positive vibes and calm demeanors from parents and coaches before, during, and after competition will also be mirrored by our athletes. If you want your child to relax, then you must relax. If you want your team to be positive, then you must be positive. If you want your players to bring the right attitude and state of mind to training and games, then you must as well. And if you want your kids to respect officials, adults, and opponents, then you must as well.

The following are some ideas to help create the right competition environment and behaviors for your children.

Know Your Role: Remember, when you attend a youth sporting event, you can be one of four things:

- A coach, who leads and organizes the athletes
- An athlete, who participates in the competition
- A fan, who cheers on the participants
- An official/referee, who applies the rules to the best of his/her ability

That's it. You cannot be more than one at the same time. Each role has certain responsibilities, and if you try to be more than one, things get messy and stress levels increase. We have all seen the Fan/Coach, aka the parent who shouts instructions, often confusing and sometimes wrong, impact negatively not only his own child but others as well. We have seen the Fan/Official, who although 75 yards from the play decides it is the wrong call even though the official is 5 yards away. And sadly, we see Coach/Referee, who instead of coaching their players decides to officiate the competition instead.

In years of speaking to audiences of middle and high school age athletes, both John and Jerry always ask, "What would you like your parents to say on the sidelines of your game?" And the answer, every single time, is a nearly unanimous chorus of "Nothing!" And if you have to say something, they say, cheer us on, but please do not coach. And no child ever has said "It's super helpful when my dad yells at the referee!"

This advice is especially hard when opposing fans, coaches, and athletes are acting inappropriately. It's hard not to engage, but rarely is it helpful. As Mark Twain said, "Never argue with an idiot. You'll never convince the idiot that you're correct, and bystanders won't be able to tell who's who." So just move away, and likely after the competition your kids will say to you, "Weren't those other parents crazy?"

Trying to play more than one role is rarely helpful, and more often than not, it's confusing and detrimental. It can be embarrassing, especially when an official or another player tells a parent to be quiet. It can also drive coach and referee dropouts. And perhaps most importantly, it takes away reps from the kids, steals learning opportunities, and robs them of decision making and autonomy. Know your role and stick to it, and the environment gets better for all involved.[18]

Be Present: Please cheer for your kids. Better yet, please cheer for all the kids out there. But don't coach. Kids want us to be present, not looking at our phones or totally uninvolved. So be on the sideline, engaged in the game, but don't be a distraction. If your child makes eye contact, give them the thumbs-up. If your child looks at you after every mistake, ask yourself, "Why do they keep looking at me—do they think they are disappointing me?" Most importantly, just be there for them. If we can tell you one thing, having watched our kids grow up in sports, time goes by very fast, and pretty soon you won't have anyone to watch anymore. So thoroughly enjoy these moments.

Model Palms Down, Not Palms Up Behaviors: We got this idea from the great Graham Betcher, the mental skills coach for UCONN

---

18 The Southern Oregon Sports Commission has developed a great toolkit and series of videos around this idea: see https://www.travelmedford.org/know-your-role.

Men's basketball's 2023 and 2024 National Championship Teams, as well as numerous NBA stars and teams. When Graham joined us on the *Way of Champions Podcast* (Episode 374), he spoke about the difference between "palms up" and "palms down" behaviors. When you are reacting to things such as bad calls, bad passes, or mistakes made by your child, and when your child is reacting to these same things, do you notice how you usually turn your palms up, bend your elbows, and yell, scream, and lose it? These are palms up behaviors, and they make you a victim. Instead of focusing on the next play, you are focused on the last one. It draws negative attention to you and rarely ever helps.

Palms down behaviors are not reactions; they are responses. They are the warriors' response. They are present- and future-focused. You cannot change the call or the play that just happened, all you can affect is the next play, and those that come after. The focus of palms down athletes is on what matters most, which is the next play. Palms down players are not victims, They are totally focused on controlling what they can control and responding to whatever comes their way.

Champion sports parents must do their utmost to be palms down at all times. If you yell, scream, complain, or micromanage your child, they will tend to do the same thing. They will become a victim. They will react and not respond. They will model what you do, not what you say. Be palms down!

Respect Officials: We have a massive officiating crisis looming in youth and high school sports. Across numerous sports in many areas, there are not even enough referees, umpires, and officials to cover existing games and competitions. In some sports, 80 to 90 percent of first-year officials do not come back for a second year because of the toxic and sometimes dangerous environment they work in. Will there be any games without the impartial judges?

It is critically important to respect our competition officials and model that behavior for our children. Yes, they will make mistakes—probably lots of them. We often forget that if your child is in a developmental phase of sports, so are the people officiating them. You are not getting a Major League umpire at your Little League game, and you are not getting a FIFA World Cup referee at your U12 soccer match. You are likely getting at least one official who is only a year or two older than the actual participants. And just as we should never yell and scream at our 10-year-old for making a mistake, we should never do the same for a kid trying to learn to referee and make a few bucks. Nor should we do it to the 50- or 60-year-old who is giving up his or her weekend so your child can play.

Next time there is a bad call, if you must say something, encourage the players on the field to shake it off and focus on the next play instead of the last one. Don't react to the bad call by fixating on it, but respond by making the next play.

Let Go of the Outcome and Enjoy the Journey: Both of us have seen our children participate in years upon years of youth, high school, and collegiate sporting events. At the time of writing this book, Jerry's children are in their 20s and 30s, and John's are about to finish high school. All of our children have had ups and downs, won championships, and suffered heartache. Some have been recognized with wonderful individual awards, and even college scholarships. And the one thing they have in common? They all have endured some bad parenting moments from their dads, and it usually always happened when the focus turned from the process to the outcome.

One thing every parent with older children will tell you is that the days are long, but the years are short and fly by so fast. You blink your eyes and your T-ball player and mini-soccer star is taller than you and playing their last high school game. We often treat this as the end of their sporting journey, but it's not. Hopefully it's simply the end of the beginning of a lifetime of activity. What we have just witnessed is but a slice of their sporting journey. Yet when we treat it as something that ends at 18 or 22, we get overly focused on the outcomes and results in the short term and lose sight of the long term.

It is very unlikely that anyone will remember the result of a youth soccer game one year from now, never mind 20 years on. If we get caught up in the moment and hyper-focused on winning today, we end up coaching from the sidelines, screaming at officials, and confronting opposing fans because only this result matters. But does it? Will it mean anything in 20 years?

Let go of today's result and just enjoy the journey. Be grateful you have a healthy child who can participate today, and even if things go poorly, ask, "What is good about this?" Sit down with your child and ask, "What is the most helpful thing I can do or say when you are competing?" Listen to their answer and respect their request. Organize a "Silent Sidelines" day for your club or league, where for one day every season, all the adults agree to stay silent. No coaching, no cheering, and certainly no yelling at officials. It's a surreal experience, but what you'll hear are the voices of the children— powerful, knowledgeable, and no longer drowned out by a sea of moms and dads. Organize a "Know Your Role" parent education session prior to the season so every parent understands the importance of knowing their role on the sidelines.

> *At your sporting events, be outcome aware,*
> *but driven by the process and purpose of sports.*
> —John O'Sullivan

Questions on the Quest

1. What was the biggest lesson you learned in this chapter, and how can you apply it?
2. What do you need to start doing (that you're not doing) to help your child compete better during competition?
3. What do you need to stop doing (that you are doing) to help your child compete better during competition?

CHAPTER 31:

WHO WANTS LUNCH?
THE BEST POST-EVENT BEHAVIORS
FOR LONG-TERM PARTICIPATION

Ninety-five percent of kids quit their sport on the ride home with their parents.
For the parents out there, be really thoughtful on how those conversations go
after practice. It shouldn't be about results-results-results. Everyone talks about
fixing the world, but I think it starts at home.

—Alex Rodriguez (A-Rod)

One of the best youth sports documentaries out there is HBO's *Trophy Kids*, an in-depth look at overbearing parents in sports that asks the viewer to contemplate whether we want what's best for our children or simply want our children to be the best. One of the most telling scenes is one where a dad is upset with his son's football performance and is giving him a harsh debrief on the ride home. The dad is angry, the son is defeated, and as his tears well up in the back seat, you know this won't end well. It's a shocking scene after which many viewers ask themselves,

"Is that what it feels like for my child?"

For far too many of us, the answer to that last question is yes, at least once in a while. Even with the best of intentions, when both parent and child are emotionally and physically exhausted after a competition, we try to make it a teachable moment. Yet our children tell us this is perhaps the least teachable moment.

It has always amazed us how a moment off the field can have such a detrimental effect, yet when we think about it, the toxicity of the ride home makes perfect sense. Emotions are high and disappointment, frustration, and exhaustion are heightened for both player and parent, yet many parents choose this moment to confront their child about a play, criticize them for having a poor game, and chastise them, their teammates, their coach, and their opponents. There could not be a less teachable moment in your child's sporting life than the ride home, yet it is often the moment that well-intentioned parents decide to do all of their teaching.

One of the biggest problems on the ride home is that a simple question from you, often meant to encourage your child, can be construed by your child as an attack on a teammate or coach. A comment such as "Why does Jenny get all the shots?" may be meant to convince your child that you think she is a good shooter who should also take shots, but this is interpreted by your daughter as "Jenny is a ball hog!" Questions such as "Why does Billy always play goalie?" or "Why does your team always play zone?" can just as easily undermine the coach's authority and again cause confusion and uncertainty for your child.

Many children have indicated that parental actions and conversations after games made them feel as though their value and worth in their parents' eyes was tied to their athletic performance and the wins and losses of their team. So ask yourself whether you are quieter after a hard loss or happier and more buoyant after a big win. Do you tend to criticize and dissect your child's performance after a loss, but overlook many of the same mistakes because he or she won? If you see that you are doing this, even though your intentions may be well meaning, your child's perceptions of your words and actions can be quite detrimental to their performance—and to your relationship.

Parents need to be a source of confidence and comfort when their child has played well in a loss, when their child has played poorly, and especially when their child has played very little or not at all. Even then, it is critically important that you do not bring up the game, as uninvited conversations may cause resentment in children. Give them the time and space to digest the game and recover physically and emotionally from a match.

When your child is ready to bring up the game and talk about it, be a quiet and reflective listener, and make sure they can see the big picture and not just the outcome of a single event. Help your child work through the game, and facilitate their growth and education by guiding them toward their own answers. Kids learn a lot when they realize things like "We had a bad week of practice, and the coach told us this was coming." Develop a consistency to the conversation by always asking these three questions:

1. What went well today?
2. What needs work?
3. What did you learn today that you can focus on in practice next week?

The only exception to the above "ride home rule" is when your child engages in behavior you would not accept at home, such as spitting, cursing, assaulting an opponent, or disrespecting a coach or authority figure. In these cases, you should initiate the conversation, not as parent to athlete, but as parent to child. Even then, you must be careful and considerate of their emotions and choose your words wisely. Deal with the issue, then put it to bed; do not use it as a segue to a discussion of the entire game.

Not every child is the same, and some children may want to discuss the game on the way home. Our advice is to let them bring it up, then let them end the conversation. If you are unsure, ask your kids whether they want to talk about the game, and honor their feelings and their position on this issue. Better still, ask them, "Who wants lunch?"

There is nothing, aside from the unacceptable behavior mentioned above, that cannot be discussed at a later time. The best part is, you will likely have a far better conversation about it hours after a game, instead of minutes.

The car ride home is so important in youth sports If after a win or loss you are obsessing about the game, what message does the child receive? It is very easy to turn a child's passion into something they dread by ending every activity with a lecture on what they could do better.
—Steve Magness, peak performance coach

Questions on the Quest

1. What was the biggest lesson you learned in this chapter, and how can you apply it?
2. What do you need to start doing (that you're not doing) to help your child have a better experience after a competition?
3. What do you need to stop doing (that you are doing) to help your child have a better experience after a competition?
4. What do you need to keep doing (that you are currently doing) to help your child unwind and recover post-competition?

Bonus Activity: Watch John's TEDx Talk "Changing the Game in Youth Sports," and be sure to always tell your kids after every competition, "I love watching you play!"[19]

---

19 https://www.youtube.com/watch?v=VXw0XGOVQvw.

CONCLUSION:

THE JOURNEY BEGINS

Every new beginning comes from some other beginning's end.

—Seneca

As we come to the end of the book, we hope you have found its stories, anecdotes, and questions helpful as you navigate the sports parenting journey. While this book may be ending, we see it as a beginning: the start of a new journey of being a champion sports parent. This is a special time in your life, one that provides you the opportunity to develop a deeper and more beautiful, connective, caring, and loving relationship with your children. In these wise words, often attributed to Winston Churchill:

> To each there comes a time in their lifetime, a special moment when they are figuratively tapped on the shoulder and offered the chance to do a very special thing. What a tragedy if that moment finds them unprepared or unqualified for that which could have been their finest hour.

In your life, being a champion sports parent is that special moment, that finest hour, and we hope we have helped to prepare you for what will be an awesome time with your youngsters. Sports is the natural venue that will serve as the path for you to practice and master the skills required to help your kids succeed in both sports and the game of life. You will be better prepared when challenging moments arise to face any obstacle, overcome any difficulty, and turn failure and setbacks into opportunities for parental and athletic growth. This book is your tool kit, and the answers you recorded as you read will enable easy reflection and revisiting of different principles as you travel the sports parenting journey.

Native American tradition teaches us about the "essential goodness" of all children. Our intention in writing this book is to help align you with this concept and make sure you are aware of how to protect, guard, and maintain this essential spirit and goodness in these young athletes, not just in sport but in all of life.

This process is delicate and is nurtured first by supporting our children's dreams and visions of what is possible. We need to convey to these great spirits that we believe in them and then sit back and watch their confidence soar as they discover the greatness within them. When you commit to the process in this book, you and your children will grow and expand to feel free, alive, energetic, and strong. Your faith in your children, reinforced within this book, will reduce anxiety, stress, and fear in times of pressure, chaos, and crisis. In a compassionate, caring, connective, and safe environment, your children will blossom.

As you will see, sports parenting is aligned with a more natural way, implementing specific truths and laws of nature that have been relied upon for centuries. With these laws, you will be more humble, kind, intuitive, and selfless. These are laws we don't need to preach like dogma but rather teach as truths because they represent the values we all believe and crave:

- Errors, mistakes, and loss cannot be avoided.
- Failures are our best teachers . . . always.
- Letting go and detachment are essential to happiness.
- Impermanence is real; nothing lasts forever.
- Patience, gratitude, and faith are virtues of natural law.
- What you resist will persist.
- You lose, yet in this way, you win.
- An opponent is actually a partner helping you to succeed.
- Soft is, indeed, strong as we watch water wear away rock.

Resistance to these laws of nature cause unnecessary suffering in sports and in life, for you as well as your children. This book will help you to flow with these natural truths. Observe what happens to a pine tree in a snowstorm. The branches fill with snow and break because they remain rigid. The willow tree branch, being flexible, bends with the weight of the snow and is able to bounce back to its original position unharmed. How is this lesson relative to your life and the sports life of your child? Notice ways that this is true for you.

To make your sports parenting journey a positive and joyful one, begin to listen and implement the lessons and messages in this book. Make it your companion when you get frustrated, annoyed, challenged, and fearful on this path. Observing and attending to these laws will help to develop unlimited personal power to influence others in a positive, productive, meaningful way.

Remember, the champion sports journey is like the river. We chose this metaphor because like the river, your path is a natural progression and flow. Your sports parenting is a journey of ups and downs, turns and surprises, cloudy and clear water. Let it flow! Commit yourself with all your heart to the courage to do what you intuitively know is the right thing to do. When this happens, you will experience profound, penetrating wisdom for parenting your children as well as navigating all aspects of your life. This is known as the "hero's journey," the path that will teach you more about yourself, parenting, and living than anything else.

To paraphrase ancient wisdom: With good sports parents, when their good work is done, the children will all feel that they have done it themselves. It's time to join and enjoy the journey!

ABOUT THE AUTHORS

Jerry Lynch and John O'Sullivan are leadership, performance, and team culture specialists. Their work has received global acclaim in youth, high school, collegiate, and professional athletics. They are highly sought after by teams, schools, and sport governing bodies around the world for their work in athletic performance, coach education, and parent engagement. Jerry and John cohost the *Way of Champions Podcast*, as well as the Way of Champions Transformational Leadership Events, and both are national advisory board members of the Positive Coaching Alliance. Their first book together, *The Champion Teammate: Timeless Lessons to Connect, Compete and Lead in Sports and Life* received international acclaim and is used by high-performing teams and athletes on the youth, high school, college and professional levels.

Jerry Lynch, PhD, is the founder and director of Way of Champions, a human potential and performance consulting group helping others master the relationship and culture-building games in athletics, business, and life. He first learned about extraordinary performance and excellence as a nationally ranked competitive athlete sponsored by Nike, running world-class times from 5,000 meters to the marathon, setting an American record in the half-marathon, and winning a national championship. He is recognized as one of the top leaders in the world in his profession. He has published 17 books in more than 10 languages. Jerry has had significant influence with Olympic sports programs from New Zealand, Germany, the Philippines, and the United

States. His work has impacted teams, coaches, and athletes in the NBA, NHL, Pro Lacrosse, and Major League Soccer, in addition to men's and women's basketball, lacrosse, field hockey, swimming, soccer, tennis, golf, and track and field at the universities of North Carolina, Duke, Maryland, California, Syracuse, Stanford, Harvard, and Middlebury. In the past 35 years alone, he has helped influence 118 world, national, conference, and state championship teams. He has had extensive media interview coverage with CBS, NBC, and PBS national television, the *New York Times*, *Oprah Magazine*, *Sports Illustrated*, *Baltimore Sun*, *Outside* magazine, and more than 400 national magazines, radio broadcasts, podcasts, and webinars. Learn more at www.WayOfChampions.com.

John O'Sullivan is the founder of Changing the Game Project, an organization dedicated to helping coaches, parents, schools, and youth sport organizations give sports back to our kids and put a little more "play" in "play ball." He is a former collegiate and professional soccer player, and has coached for more than 30 years on the youth, high school, and collegiate levels. John has written two bestselling books, *Changing the Game* and *Every Moment Matters*, and his work has appeared on CNN, *Outside* magazine, *Huffington Post*, *Boston Globe*, ESPN, NBC Sports, and numerous other media outlets. He has consulted with the USOC, US Soccer, USA Swimming, US Ski and Snowboard, USA Wrestling, Ireland Rugby, National Rugby League of Australia, the PGA, and many other entities, including teams and coaches at Ohio State, Rutgers, Fordham, Colby, and USF. You can learn more at www. ChangingTheGameProject.com.

For bulk orders of our books *The Champion Sports Parent* or *The Champion Teammate,* please email John@ChangingTheGameProject.com

FOR FURTHER READING

Books by Jerry Lynch

The Champion Teammate
Thinking Body, Dancing Mind
Way of the Champion
The Competitive Buddha
Win the Day
Everyday Champion Wisdom
Coaching with Heart
Let Them Play
Spirit of the Dancing Warrior
Working Out Working Within
Tao Mentoring
Creative Coaching

Books by John O'Sullivan

The Champion Teammate
Changing the Game
Every Moment Matters
Is it Wise to Specialize?